D1546293

Update service available

Keeping ahead of the sportscard counterfeiters is a never-ending challenge. New forgeries have been discovered at an average rate of at least one per month for the past two years or more. There is no reason to believe that pace will slacken in the near future.

Only through the provision of timely information to dealers, collectors and investors can the sale of counterfeit cards be halted. With the market diminished, the incentive to issue counterfeit cards may also disappear.

The addition of several newly discovered counterfeits as this edition went to press (see Pages 142-151) points up the need for a continuing source of fast, accurate information.

For this reason, the publisher of this book is offering buyers the opportunity to subscribe to an update service on an annual basis.

As new counterfeits are discovered during the course of the year, information and photographs will be assembled in format similar to the listings within this book. These updates will be compiled in looseleaf form and mailed to subscribers immediately upon publication, allowing the purchaser of this book to have continuing access to up-to-the-minute data on current counterfeits.

Cost of this update service is just $10 per calendar year. Persons who subscribe to the service after the beginning of the year will receive all updates published to that point, plus all future updates through the end of the calendar year.

Use the coupon below or a reasonable facsimile to sign up now for this valuable service. Remember, the information in just a single new listing can save you several times the cost of the entire year's subscription.

_____ Yes, I want to keep informed on new counterfeit discoveries, please enter my subscription to your update service for calendar 1992. I enclose $10.

_____ Please enroll me to receive all 1993 counterfeit updates, as well. I enclose an additional $10.

Make checks payable to **Krause Publications** and mail to:
Counterfeit Book Updates
700 E. State St.
Iola, WI 54990

Name _____

Address _____

City _____ State _____ ZIP _____

Sportscard Counterfeit Detector

By the staff of Sports Collectors Digest
and
The National Association of Sportscard
Dealers and Manufacturers (NASDAM)

Bob Lemke, editor

Acknowledgements

The editor wishes to thank the many dealers, collectors and other hobbyists who provided information and examination specimens for the compilation of this book. Special thanks go to the board of directors and members of NASDAM for their efforts — most especially to Sally Grace, who spearheaded the group's participation and co-ordinated its efforts with those of the SCD staff. Hobbyists who provided special assistance include: Steve Barcus, Rob Berg, David Berman, Guy Blasco, Gary Brison, George Brown, Cardtime Wholesalers, Dan Cook, Lou Costanzo, Greg Czerkies, David Denenberg, Terry Diener, Don Dorwart Jr., Ned Fishkin, Gary Gagen, Tony Galovich, Vince Grisi, John Inouye, Joe Irmen, Ted Isham, John Lockwood, Roger Marth, Jim McLauchlin, Mike O'Brien, Bud Obermeyer, Wally Opyt, Bill Rodman, Rut's Baseball Cards, Ferdi Tan, Randy Thompson and Henry Yee.

ISBN: 0-87341-194-3
Library of Congress: 91-77563

Published by

Table of contents

Preface

The detection of counterfeit sportscards — while it can and should employ some scientific procedures — is not an exact science. To be consistently correct requires a unique combination of training and experience.

Foremost is exposure to sportscards themselves. When a person has long or intensive exposure to all types of cards — new and old; baseball, football, basketball and hockey — he quickly develops a sense (perhaps even subconsciously) of the characteristics of each card. When a card comes along that is not quite "right," in terms of printing quality, weight and feel of the cardboard or surface texture, an experienced card handler often hears alarm bells.

Too often, however, the viewer of such a card cannot specifically pinpoint what is wrong with the card that identifies it as a counterfeit rather than just a printing variation or abnormality. It is here that training and/or experience in the printing methods by which cards are produced — and illegally reproduced — is necessary. A successful counterfeit detector must have an understanding of today's complex computerized printing technology as well as the literally stone-age lithography techniques by which cards were produced for the tobacco companies 80 years ago.

Finally, formal training in the field of counterfeit detection is beneficial. Knowing the specific methods by which a counterfeit is created from a genuine item defines the perimeter of the battleground where this war is fought. Understanding the physiology of the counterfeit and the psychology of the counterfeiter is essential to detection.

I began collecting sportscards in 1954 and have been involved daily in the sportscard hobby on a professional basis for more than a decade. Nearly 20 years in the publishing business have imparted a thorough working knowledge of the graphic arts and printing technology. A graduate of the American Numismatic Association's counterfeit detection training program, I have written numerous articles on counterfeit currency and counterfeit sportscards.

While this book is the result of dedicated work on the part of many persons in the hobby/industry, I alone must accept the responsibility for the final product. While I am confident that what is presented here is accurate, if there are mistakes in the attribution of counterfeit status or within the specific descriptions of counterfeit cards, they are my errors. It is fervently hoped that the reader will assist the on-going work by providing correction to my mistakes and by filling the many informational and photographic gaps within these pages.

Bob Lemke
January, 1992

A special note
about this edition . . .

You hold in your hands the first edition of the *Sportscard Counterfeit Detector*. It must be recognized that this edition is not "complete." In a larger sense, this book will never be complete because it is the publisher's intention to keep the volume perpetually in print and updated as new counterfeits are discovered.

Your assistance is vital

The assistance of all readers is particularly sought to help narrow the gap toward completeness on this project. Specifically, if any reader can assist in providing information and/or specimens of counterfeit cards not listed in this book, or for listings which are incomplete in this edition, or information on errors which might be promulgated in these pages, they are urged to contact: Bob Lemke, Sports Collectors Digest, 700 E. State St., Iola, WI 54990.

Remember, it was the assistance of your fellow dealers and collectors that made possible the creation of this book. One day the information which they unselfishly provided could prevent you from making a mistake worth several hundred or several thousand dollars. Please be as generous with your information for the greater benefit of the entire hobby/industry.

The scope of this book

Comprehensive coverage within the pages of this book is limited to counterfeit versions of genuine sportscards. The scope of this edition does not allow for the inclusion of detailed data concerning reprints (other than those made for the specific purpose of defrauding buyers), fantasy cards or unauthorized collector issues ("broders"), although those areas are covered in brief chapters in this volume.

All counterfeits known to the editor at presstime are presented in this book, including some cards for which few details are currently available. It is the intention of the publisher to continually update the body of this work as new information becomes available.

A cautionary note . . .

Just because a card is not listed in this book does not mean it is not a counterfeit. This book lists all counterfeits which were known to a relatively small group of hobby professionals, and for which definitive data could be worked up within a tight production schedule. There are undoubtedly counterfeit cards in the hobby market that are unlisted here. It is hoped the professional reader will be able to use the methodology learned here and apply it to the examination of other suspect cards.

How to use this book

This book cannot detect counterfeit sportscards for you. It does indicate which counterfeits were known to the publisher at the time of printing, and how the editors determined the cards were counterfeit. The final determination of whether a suspect card is good or bad rests in your hands.

You can count on this — if a card you hold displays the characteristics for that specific counterfeit, it *is* a counterfeit. It cannot be genuine, no matter how much you paid for it, nor how much you wish it to be genuine. Conversely, just because a card you suspect does not display the specific characteristics shown in this book does not mean it cannot be a counterfeit. The fakers will continue to produce new counterfeits of cards which had not previously been reproduced, and they will continue to produce new versions of cards which have already been counterfeited. Hopefully, by studying the methods by which existing counterfeits have been identified in this book, you can apply that knowledge to a suspect card you might be faced with that is not currently covered in this volume.

To have any chance at all of matching a suspect card with the known fakes in this book, it is essential that you get a good magnifying glass. Virtually all of the counterfeits in this book can be identified with a lens no stronger than 5X (producing an image five times actual size), since we have already pinpointed the areas in which to conduct a close-up examination. For a few cards, a lens in the range to 10X might be desirable, but for the average dealer or collector, nothing stronger will ever be needed. While the initial efforts to identify characteristics of many of these counterfeits included the use of a stereo microscope, scales which weigh to tenths of a gram and other laboratory-quality instruments, the expense of such equipment is totally unnecessary to fully utilize the information in this book.

Each known counterfeit is exposed in this book through written descriptions and — where available — comparative photographs. Some examples, however, are not completely presented due to a lack of either actual specimens of the counterfeits, of the genuine cards, or both. Unless otherwise marked, the full front and back card photos are of the specific counterfeit being profiled. Where possible, microphotographs of both genuine and counterfeit cards are presented. Generally these detail photos provide the easiest clue to identification. Other characteristics of the counterfeits will appear in the text. It should be noted that not all of the identified characteristics of the counterfeits have been presented. This was done both to conserve space and to avoid letting the counterfeiters know all of the mistakes they made in attempting to reproduce the genuine cards.

We have generally avoided the use of subjective signposts to positively identify counterfeits. Such things as shade and intensity of color and ink coverage, clarity of photo, texture of the cardboard stock and composition of the color printing dot structure are subject to the interpretation of the viewer and cannot be easily imparted in the written word nor even in the finest of photographs. For that reason, we have concentrated on presenting, wherever possible, tell-tale clues that can be found on each and every specimen of a particular counterfeit card and on no known specimens of the genuine card.

The emphasis in this book's presentation has been on ease of use for the reader. Suggestions for improvement are invited by the editor.

A word about weight . . .

With fewer than a handful of exceptions, of the more than 100 types of counterfeit sportscards covered in this book, none weigh in within the tolerances to be expected for the genuine cards they purport to be.

In most cases, a broad approximation of the paper stock on which the genuine cards were printed is the best that a counterfeiter can provide for his product. In virtually all cases, this cardboard, when imprinted and cut to the size of the real thing, will be so significantly heavier or lighter that it provides the first clue to a card's counterfeit status. That difference in weight is seldom less than 3-4%, most often 5-10%, but occasionally as much as 20% or more.

Unfortunately, it takes a very sensitive (and very expensive) scale, weighing differences as little as one-tenth of a gram, to provide this data. For this reason, we have not, in most cases, included weight information as the basis for identifying the counterfeits in this book.

Other, more pragmatic reasons mitigate against quoting specific weights either for genuine or counterfeit cards. First and foremost, a weight recorded on a scale at the publisher's office may be different than a weight recorded at your location. Differences in the calibration of scales and the interpretation of the reading by the person doing the weighing are sure to exist. Outside of laboratory conditions, most scales will weigh the very same item differently at different times, depending on such variables as drafts within the room and other physical conditions. Too, except for the most recent cards in Mint condition, wear and aging factors have to be considered in the weight of genuine cards, as well as the possibility that slight differences in "batches" of cardboard may have existed at the time of printing. Counterfeits, because of the less exact nature of their manufacture are sure to vary in weight more from card to card than genuine examples. Because our investigation was not conducted on large numbers of specimens of any given counterfeit, any weights quoted would not be sufficiently representative.

In the real hobby world, the weight of a card can never be used in and of itself to determine whether a card is genuine or counterfeit. It should only be considered as a relative measure. If you have a good balance scale, keep a file of the weight range of genuine cards of a specific issue. In most cases you'll find suprisingly little variance. If you ever have cause to weigh a suspect card, and it falls outside of your recorded range, that should be an immediate indicator that further investigation is necessary.

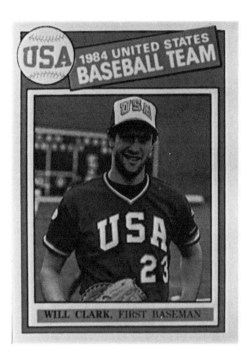

Fantasies and "broders"

Only a few of the cards which fit the broad category of "collectors' issues" could even remotely qualify for inclusion in the main body of this book.

Instead, a few words about the genre will probably be sufficient.

While there were dozens of collectors' issues produced in the 1970s, they were principally team sets of non-current players, done in designs that had no resemblance to contemporary cards.

A phenomenon of the 1980s was the emergence of current-player cards that have come to be known by the generic term of "broders," in honor of the person who was responsible for the issue of the majority of such cards through the middle years of the decade.

By definition, broders are cards that are not licensed by the player depicted, the players' association or the league. With no licenses to restrict them, there is no control over the number of cards issued. Theoretically, if a particular broder sells well, the card could be reprinted — either by the original issuer or anybody else. This means that such cards have no true collector value. In general, however, until recent years many of the broder cards were of better design and better quality printing than the cards of the major legal manufacturers. Selling for 25¢ to $1 apiece, they were (and still are) attractive alternatives to high-priced "real" cards of currently hot superstars — at least among children and beginning collectors.

In the mid-1980s, Krause Publications became the first hobby entity to take a stand against broders, refusing to accept advertising for the cards. Other publications have followed suit in recent years.

Until very recently, the persons who should have shouldered the responsibility for controling the spread of these pirate cards were totally indifferent to the problem. The players' unions and leagues, to whom legitimate card manufacturers pay royalties for the use of player pictures and team logos, should have been tracking down the makers of these cards and halting their printing presses. Led by the National Basketball Association, beginning in 1990, at least a token effort is now being made to crack down on the illegal cards.

Still, new broders appear each month and it is not uncommon at card shows to find dealer tables occupied entirely by unauthorized issues. These cards will not disappear until other elements of the hobby take action. If card show promoters would refuse to allow broders to be displayed or sold, the market for such cards would disappear. In today's ever competitive hobby market, however, show promoters in most cities cannot afford to do anything that will drive paying tableholders to another promoter's show, so it is unlikely that broders will become an endangered species anytime soon.

The co-sponsors of this book, the National Association of Sportscard Dealers and Manufacturers (NASDAM) does not allow broders to be sold at shows which it sanctions, and its by-laws prohibit its members from dealing in unauthorized issues. A similar stand has been taken by the other major dealers' organization, the Sports Collectibles Association International (SCAI).

A recent trend among the producers of broders has been to issue cards in similitude to genuine card designs. After Michael Jordan's well publicized visit to the Chicago White Sox batting cage, this resulted in Michael Jordan baseball cards being produced in the designs of the 1986 Topps and Donruss cards, and even a card shared with Bo Jackson in the design of the 1986 Fleer "Major League Prospects" design.

Similarly, Nolan Ryan, who originally shared his 1968 Topps card with Jerry Koosman, can be found on a recent broder all by himself in a design that

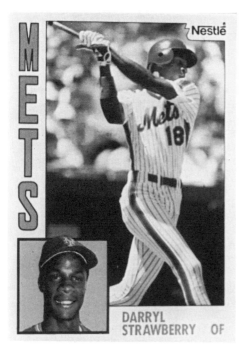
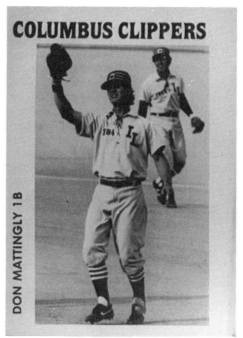

Left: Black-and-white versions of the star cards from the 1984 Topps/Nestle's issue can be found purporting to be rare proof cards. Right: Don Mattingly in a 19th Century uniform is found on this common fantasy issue.

WAYNE GRETZKY
Indianapolis Racers - 1978

The makers of this Wayne Gretzky fantasy sent out a mailing trying to convince dealers it was a genuine 1978 issue.

reproduces the burlap look of the '68 Topps. Other oft-seen cards of this type depict Will Clark in the 1984 U.S. Olympic team uniform, and done in the style of the 1985 Topps cards which depicted eligible players from that squad, and a Darryl Strawberry card done in the style of a 1984 TCMA Tidewater Tides issue.

The class of unauthorized cards which comes the closest to fitting the scope of this book is the fantasies. These are cards that are generally, but not always, produced several years after the originals in an attempt to induce the belief that they are real cards that have somehow been overlooked by the entire hobby.

Don Mattingly has been a frequent victim of these fantasy cards. There have been fantasy cards depicting him as an Evansville High School player and as a member of the Greensboro Hornets minor league team. One widely circulated card is done in a style roughly similar to a 1982 TCMA card; it depicts Mattingly in a 19th Century uniform used for a special game.

A recent fantasy card was offered depicting Wayne Gretzky in the uniform of the Indianapolis Racers, and purporting to have been issued in 1978, and carries the copyright line of "National Sports Cards".

Still another type of fantasy card that was popular a couple of years back was the phony "proof card" and "test issue". Done in black-and-white (it's much cheaper to print than a color fake), these cards attempt to portray rare pre-production versions of valuable cards. Such fantasies are usually found with notations of "TEST" or "PROOF" overprinted on them, along with some meaningless code combinations of letters and/or numbers. The producers of such cards are apparently unaware that genuine card manufacturers would never have cause to make such proof cards — or at least they hope the suckers to whom they're trying to sell the phony proofs are ignorant about actual printing methods.

Two frequently seen types of this fakery are black-and-white versions of the 1984 Topps-printed Nestle's cards, and the infamous 1989 Fleer card of Billy Ripken which features a vulgarism visible on the knob of his bat.

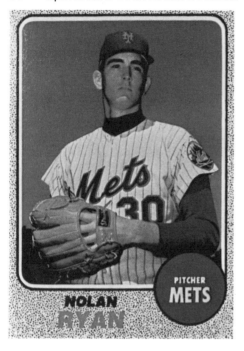

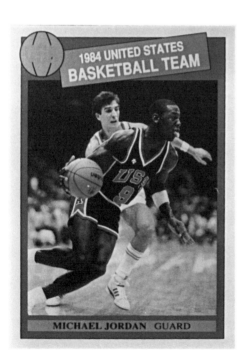

Each new superstar that emerges in big time sports can expect to find his image pirated by makers of illegal "broder" cards. First it was Don Mattingly and Wade Boggs, then Jose Canseco and Bo Jackson, then Michael Jordan and Nolan Ryan, now it's Frank Thomas and Eric Lindros.

Reprints

It is a fine line indeed which separates a reprint from a counterfeit.

Both are reproductions of a genuine sportscard produced for profit. It is largely the degree of profitability being sought by the second-generation manufacturer that marks the difference. The reprinter seeks to create a replica card of sufficient similitude to the genuine to entice purchasers who cannot find or afford the real card. Generally the selling price of a reprint is set based upon the actual costs of the manufacturer. The counterfeiter seeks to create a replica card that is so similar to the genuine as to entice purchasers into believing they are purchasing the original. The selling price of a counterfeit is generally based on the current hobby market value of the genuine card.

Intent, therefore, seems to be the key to differentiating an innocent reprint from a sinister forgery.

That is the criteria upon which decisions were made to include or exclude certain unauthentic cards from the body of this work. Usually, a person who intends his replica cards to be sold as reprints builds into his creation at least one significant difference between the reproduction and the original. It may be as dramatic and indisputable as varying the size of the reproduction, or the color of

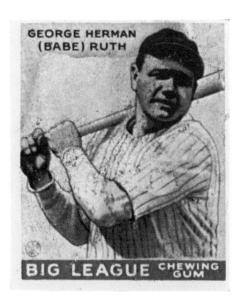 

This 1933 Goudey Babe Ruth reproduction was printed as an innocent substitute for the collector who could not afford the real thing. It was subsequently altered by having the "Reprint" notation erased and being artificially aged with dirt and stains to give it the appearance of a 50-year-old card. It was sold as genuine to an unsuspecting buyer.

ink with which the card backs are printed. It may be as simple as adding the word "Reprint" in tiny — easily removed — type on the back of the card. Often the differences are more subtle variances from the original's cardboard stock and surface finish.

The counterfeiter, by contrast, does everything possible to make his product as much like the genuine as possible.

The reader will notice several cards listed in this book that are clearly marked as reprints. It is the editor's contention that these cards — despite the reprint disclaimer — were produced with the intention of defrauding the hobby. As often as not, specimens of these cards that are seen in the marketplace have had the word "Reprint" erased. The similarity of paper stock and printing quality, at least as viewed by non-expert hobbyists, to the genuine cards makes this series of reprints a danger that warrants their inclusion here.

Conversely, a veteran hobbyist may note the absence from these listings of some early reprint cards which bore no notation of their status. While those who know well the Michigan dealer who was responsible for the production of many such cards in the early 1970s may question his motivations in producing unmarked reprints, it is clear that within the hobby — such as it existed at that time — the reproductions were not a danger. As is so often the case with unmarked reprints, however, these early replicas soon found their way into the hands of the "public," being passed as genuine. They continue to surface today in "old-time" collections, much to the consternation of the would-be seller.

Obviously, that is the principal danger of sports card reprints — that they will be altered by unscrupulous persons who will attempt to sell them to the unwary as originals. This is usually accomplished by erasing or covering up the reprint notation, if any, which appears on the back of the card, and by artifically ageing the card through the judicious application of dirt, or even weak solutions of tea or coffee. The altered reprints are usually offered for sale with a convincing story about how they have been in the family for generations. The price is almost always quoted at a great discount from current catalog value, hoping to prey on the greed of a buyer who thinks he is getting a real steal of a deal.

The reprinting of sportscards was unknown until about 20 years ago. After all, until that time, cards had little or no monetary value. They were children's toys that were seriously collected by only a handful of adults who preferred trading the cards to buying and selling.

Since the floodgates of reprinting were opened in the early 1970s with the reproduction of a handful of Hall of Famers from the 1933 and 1934 Goudey sets and a few others, the torrent has not yet subsided. A large percentage of the major baseball card issues from the pre-World War II years have been reprinted in whole or in part, along with a significant sampling of the national, regional and local issues of the late 1940s and 1950s. Only the existence of copyright laws has prevented major reprintings of more recent cards. Until very recently, football, basketball and other sports cards were ignored by reprinters; again, because of lack of collector value of the originals.

Reprints are usually sold as complete sets. A price of 10¢ per card is not uncommon, and some sets that have utilized high-gloss finish cost even more. In the 1970s and 1980s, many reprints were sold in books, which had the cards perforated for easy removal. Many of the cards are still found with perforated edges, though they can also be found with the ragged edges trimmed. It is from these books that many of the reprints of single Hall of Famer cards originated.

It is beyond the scope of this book to fully detail all of the reprints which have been produced in the past two decades, though perhaps future editions may be more complete in that respect.

For now, we will provide an outline of the more commonly encountered baseball card reprints, along with a few notes. This list should not be considered complete, as some earlier issues may have been overlooked, and new reprints of older sets are appearing at the rate of one every couple of months or so.

The parenthetical designations are the *American Card Catalog* numbers of the original issues, where appropriate.

1869 Cincinnati Red Stockings team card
1887 Lone Jack cigarettes
All 13 cards of the 1886 champion St. Louis Browns have been reprinted.

1887-88 Allen & Ginter (N28, N29, N43)
1888 Goodwin Champions (N162)
All of the baseball players from the multi-sport composition of these sets have been reprinted; some by more than one manufacturer.

1887-1890 Old Judge/Gypsy Queen (N172)
All of the Hall of Famers and many other players from this landmark set have been reprinted in one of several replica reissues.

1895 Mayo Cut Plug (N300)
The major league baseball player cards and the college football player cards from this issue have all been reprinted.

1904 Fan Craze (WG2)
The 51-card American League and 48-card National League game card sets have been fully reprinted.

1909 Ramly (T204)
The complete set of this elegant 121 card issue has been reprinted.

1909-11 American Tobacco Co. (T206)
Single cards — including the "King of Baseball Cards," Honus Wagner — have been oft reprinted. Two different companies have offered reprints of the entire set — 524 cards.

1910 American Tobacco Co. (T205)
The complete set of 208 cards has been reprinted, as have been selected single cards.

1911 Mecca doublefolders (T201)
The complete set of 50 cards has been reprinted.

1911 Turkey Reds (T3)
The 100 baseball player cards from this large-format set (the originals were 5¾x8") have been reprinted in modern 2½x3½" size. These Turkey Red "minis" are sometimes seen with the reprint notice on the back erased and the cards artifically "aged," being sold as rare prototypes.

1912 Hassan triplefolders (T202)
The complete set of this issue has been reprinted.

1913 Fatima team cards (T200)
All 16 major league team cards have been reprinted.

1913 Tom Barker National Game (WG5)
The 52 game cards were reprinted as a set.

1914-15 Cracker Jack
Single cards of the 1914 (set of 144) and 1915 (set of 176) have been reprinted, as has the complete 1915 set.

1915 Sporting News
This 200-card set has been reprinted in its entirety.

1916 Collins-McCarthy (E135)
All 200 cards reprinted.

1921 American Caramel Co. (E121)
Selected star cards reprinted.

1922 American Caramel Co. (E120)
A complete reprint of the 240-card set has been produced.

1922 strip cards (W551)
Selected Hall of Famers reprinted.

1925 strip cards (W504)
16 Brooklyn Dodgers players and a team card reprinted.

1926 strip cards (W512)
Selected Hall of Famers reprinted.

1927 playing cards (W560)
A complete-set reprint.

1928 Tharp's ice cream
Various star cards reprinted.

1928 Babe Ruth candy
Card #2 of the six-card set reprinted.

1931 Babe Ruth Sportoscope flip book

1933 Tattoo Orbit
Selected Hall of Famers reprinted.

1933 DeLong
Complete set of 24 cards reprinted.

1933 Goudey premium
Four large-format cards reprinted.

1933 Goudey

1933 Goudey Sport Kings

1934-36 Diamond Stars

1934 Goudey

1935 Goudey four-in-one

1935 National Chicle (football)

1936 Goudey game

1938 Goudey heads-up

1939 Play Ball—America

1940 Play Ball

1941 Play Ball

1941 Goudey
Each of the above 12 sets has been reproduced in their entirety; some more than once. In addition, most of the Hall of Fame players from these sets have been reproduced as individual reprints.

1946-50 Remar bread
Selected star cards from this Pacific Coast League series reprinted.

1947 Tip Top
Complete 163-card reprint.

1947-48 Jackie Robinson ad cards
Cards from a Montreal clothier and Old Gold cigarettes have been reprinted in postcard size.

1947-66 Exhibit cards
Selected star cards reprinted.

1948 Sport Thrills
Complete set reprint.

1948 Bowman
The black-and-white baseball card set of 48 cards has been reprinted in its entirety, along with the 108-card football issue and 72-card basketball set.

1948-49 Leaf
Selected star player cards reprinted.

1949 Bowman
Both the 240-card set of major league players and the rare 36-card Pacific

Coast League player issue have been reprinted in their entirety.

1950 Bowman

Only selected stars from this 252-card issue have been reproduced.

1951 Bowman

1952 Bowman

The above two sets have been reprinted both as individual cards and as complete boxed sets with modern glossy surface finish.

1952 Topps

Virtually the complete 407-card set was reprinted in the current smaller 2½x3½" format as a boxed set by Topps.

1953 Bowman color

1953 Bowman black-and-white

Both sets have been reprinted in their entirety.

1953 Topps

The complete set, along with some cards that weren't part of the original issue, was reprinted in 1991 in a smaller-format glossy version.

☆　☆　☆

The following regional baseball card sets have been reprinted in their entirety. Most of them have been altered in format from their original sizes to conform to the now-standard 2½x3½" size.

1952 Red Man tobacco

1953 Johnston cookies

1954 Red Heart dog food

1954 Dan-Dee potato chips

1954 Wilson Franks

1954 Johnston cookies

1955 Johnston cookies

1955 Rodeo meats

1956 Rodeo meats

1957 Spic-and-Span

1959 Home Run Derby

1960 Lake to Lake milk

1968 Dexter Press/Coca Cola

Star cards reprinted in 2½x3¼" sticker format.

1970 Flavor-est milk

A reprint of an unauthorized collectors issue!

☆　☆　☆

Even minor league cards have not been safe from reprinting. More than a dozen of the original TCMA minor league cards of the 1979-1985 era were reprinted and sold as part of 100-card collector packages. The reprints are distinguishable from the originals by the existence on the back of Major League Baseball logos and/or on the front by the existence of white borders which are not found on the originals. The reprinted minor league cards are:

1979 Kelvin Chapman, Tidewater

1979 Ron Hassey, Tacoma

1980 Tom Foley, Waterbury

1980 Matt Galante, Columbus

1981 Michael Cole, Wisconsin Rapids

1983 Jack Fimple, Albuquerque

1983 Kirk McCaskill, Redwood

1983 Spike Owen, Salt Lake City

1984 Rufino Linares, Richmond

1984 Frank Wills, Omaha

1984 Kurt Stillwell, Cedar Rapids

1985 Paul Assenmacher, Durham

1985 Jeff Dedmon, Richmond

1985 Tom Filer, Syracuse

Alterations

Counterfeits are not the only bogus cards that hobbyists must be wary of. The alteration of genuine cards to make them appear to be a more valuable variation is also a danger.

That threat became reality in the summer of 1990 when altered versions of two of the hobby's most expensive cards began appearing. The cards were the "MAGIE" spelling error and the "DOYLE, N.Y. NAT'L" variation from the T206 American Tobacco Co. set of 1909-11.

The Magie card has a long history as one of the most desirable cards in the "old-time" hobby's most popular set. A misspelling of the name of Phillies outfielder Sherry Magee was quickly corrected when the T206 cards were first issued, creating a scarce variation. In the summer of 1990, a "Magie" error card in Excellent condition was valued at $7,500.

Even more valuable was the Doyle "Nat'l" variation. Uncovered nearly a decade ago, but kept secret while the discoverer attempted to find additional speci-

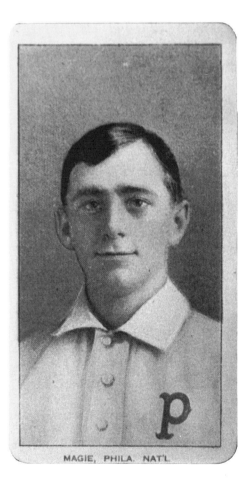

MAGIE, PHILA. NAT'L   DOYLE, N. Y. NAT'L

By altering the line of type at the bottom of these cards, a $200 pair of common versions was fraudulently transformed into $20,000 worth of fake rarities.

mens, fewer than a handful of genuine examples were known in the summer of 1990, making it numerically much rarer than even the famed Honus Wagner card from the same set.

There were four Doyle card types issued in the T206 set. Three were of N.Y. Giants second baseman Larry Doyle in portrait, batting and throwing poses; the fourth was of Giants pitcher Judd "Slow Joe" Doyle, shown winding up to pitch. Virtually all of the known cards of Judd Doyle omit the league designation in the line of type at the bottom of the card, leaving just "DOYLE, N.Y.".

In the summer of 1990, the few known examples of the leagueless variation were valued at $15,000 in Excellent condition.

The value of these variations was too much temptation for one sharp operator who began buying up specimens of the genuine, lower-valued variations of these cards. In Excellent condition, a Magee or a Doyle, Nat'l T206 would sell for under $100. The genuine cards were then altered by erasing the line of type at the bottom and replacing it with an entirely new line, creating a bogus example of the rare variations. The style of type chosen and the color of ink were virtual perfect matches, but the fakers made one fatal flaw in not exactly copying the style of league designation on the cards.

On all genuine T206 National League cards, the "N" of "NAT'L" is significantly larger than the other three letters, and the top of the apostrophe is flush with the tops of the letters "ATL". On the altered cards, the "N" was reproduced the same size as the other letters, and the top of the apostrophe was allowed to rise above the tops of the letters.

By the time the story of these fakes was printed in *Sports Collectors Digest*, two of the Doyles and one of the Magies had been sold to unsuspecting collectors. As of the end of 1991, no further examples have been found.

Thankfully, there are few similar rare cards in the hobby which can be simulated by altering a genuine less-expensive specimen. Also, the recent trend among collectors away from paying big dollars for variations works against the possibilities of more forgeries of this type being created.

Collectors and dealers, however, must be wary of the potential for such fraud.

Genuine   **Altered**

On a genuine T206 National Leaguer's card, the "N" is larger than the "ATL" and the apostrophe is level with the tops of the last three letters. The altered cards show the "N" the same size as the other letters, and the top of the apostrophe floats above the tops of the letters.

The manufacturers

Between the early 1980s, when a pair of Southern Californians were prosecuted for selling counterfeit 1963 Topps Pete Rose rookie cards, and 1991, when both Topps and Leaf-Donruss launched major investigations into counterfeiting rings, there was not a single known case of a person being arrested for either counterfeiting or selling counterfeit cards, and only a couple of instances on record in which persons were required to make restitution for selling fakes.

The plain fact was that the legitimate card companies did not seem interested in protecting the hobby from counterfeiters. The attitude among the manufacturers seemed to be that they had made their profit from the cards' sale originally, and they were no longer concerned with those cards in the aftermarket.

Perhaps the investigations launched in 1991 were a sign that at least some of the card companies were willing to participate in cleaning up this problem.

The first indication that a major card company recognized the counterfeiting problem and was willing to do something about it came in the summer of 1988, when Upper Deck announced its forthcoming 1989 premiere baseball card set. One of the principal characteristics on which Upper Deck pre-sold their new premium card concept was that the card would be counterfeit-proof. The application of a hologram to each card was intended to insure that Upper Deck cards could never be illegally duplicated. The expense of creating and printing a duplicate hologram is theoretically too great for counterfeiters to shoulder.

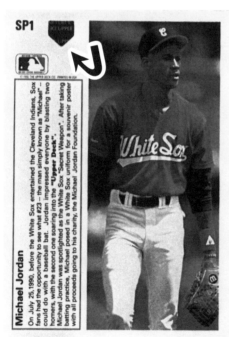

So far, Upper Deck's technology seems to be working. There are no known cases of Upper Deck cards having been counterfeited.

In late 1991, two other major manufacturers announced their own anti-counterfeiting measures.

With the introduction of its Pinnacle football set, Score debuted a small optical variable device on the back which they claim cannot be reproduced by the techniques employed by counterfeiters. The specially designed strip shows one image when it is viewed through a special ribbed plastic tool laid horizontally on the card, and a different image when the tool is laid vertically on the card.

Score has promised to incorporate this technology on its future card issues.

Donruss has also premiered an anti-counterfeiting measure on its new upscale 1992 baseball card issue. A special application of a fifth-color ink on the back of the card creates another optical variable device that would be difficult or impossible to duplicate. The printing thus applied can only be seen when the card is held at a very specific and narrow range of angles.

Hot-stamped holograms on the backs of its cards have so far protected Upper Deck from counterfeiters.

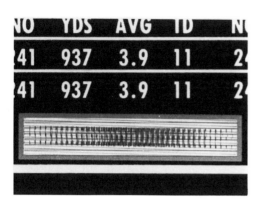

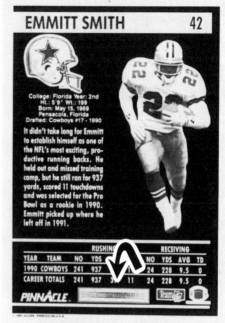

A special optical variable bar printed on the backs of Score's new Pinnacle football cards, and promised for future issues of other cards, is said to be impossible to counterfeit.

The hobby can only hope that other card companies will invest the time, technology and money necessary to protect their products' integrity — and more importantly — their customers.

Based on the response to a survey of major card companies conducted prior to the publication of this book, however, there is not much reason to be optimistic about future anti-counterfeiting measures.

Surveys were sent to 22 card manufacturers. Only 11 companies responded.

Each of the companies was asked: 1) Whether they provide an authentication service to collectors or dealers who suspect they may have counterfeit versions of the company's cards; 2) If the company is interested in receiving reports of persons selling counterfeit versions of their products; 3) If the company has ever taken civil or criminal action against those making or selling counterfeits, and, 4) Whether they would take such action if warranted in the future.

Those responses are summarized here, in no particular order of manufacturer:

Pacific Trading Cards Inc., 18424 Highway 99, Lynwood, WA 98037

The company does not offer an authentication service to the hobby, but would be interested in receiving reports of persons selling counterfeits. They have not had to take action against counterfeiters in the past but would do so if necessary in the future.

Impel Marketing Inc., P.O. Box 14930, Research Triangle Park, NC 27709

The company offers authentication service and solicits reports of counterfeit sales addressed to its Consumer Relations Department. Donald Fish, senior vice president - sports marketing, indicated his company and certain of its licensors, "have investigated and pursued counterfeiting allegations in the past," usually resulting in their being resolved without resort to legal actions. Under appropriate circumstances, according to the spokesman, they would consider civil or criminal pursuit in future cases which might arise.

Goal Line Art., Inc., P.O. Box 372, Ridley Park, PA 19078

The company seeks information on suspected counterfeit cards and will authenticate suspected cards. Address inquiries to M. Mazziotta at the address above or phone (215) 532-9415. The company has not yet had to take action against counterfeiters but a spokesman said, "All such criminal activities will be taken seriously and handled accordingly."

Star Pics Inc., 7125 Orchard Lake Rd., Suite 300, West Bloomfield, MI 48322

A Star Pics spokesman said, "We are looking into a more sophisticated method to handle (counterfeit) inquiries, but at this time Customer Service should be contacted. We have taken considerable steps to ensure the authenticity of our randomly inserted autograph cards, and would be especially interested if someone suspects a problem in this area." Inquiries should be directed to R.M. Rylko at the address above. Rylko noted Star Pics has no current action underway in the civil or criminal systems but, "we will always protect SPI and the hobby whenever there is a reason to believe that anyone is manufacturing and distributing illegal/unauthorized material."

Fleer Corp., Tenth and Somerville,Philadelphia, PA 19141

Fleer has provided and will continue to provide authentication services with reference to suspected counterfeit Fleer cards. Inquiries about counterfeits and reports of persons involved in the sale of suspected counterfeit Fleer cards should be directed to: Warren Hensley, Director of Security, at the address above. According to Fleer president Vincent J. Murray, "Fleer has cooperated, and will continue to cooperate, with individuals, dealers or civil authorities in pursuing criminal charges against any person counterfeiting our product." He added, "Fleer will vigorously prosecute future cases depending on the merits of each incident."

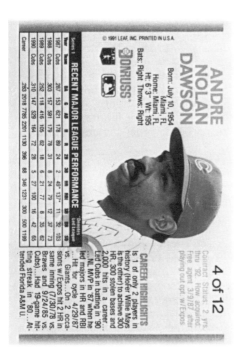

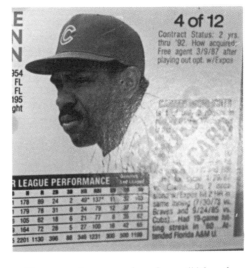

Donruss has employed a fifth-color overprint on the backs of its 1992 baseball cards to foil counterfeiters. Visible only at certain angles, the technique cannot be cheaply duplicated by counterfeiters.

Jogo Inc., 1872 Queensdale Ave., Glouchester Ontario K1T 1K1

Company officials said they have never been contacted about any suspected counterfeits of its product, but would welcome inquiries addressed to John Bradley at the address above, or contacts by phone at (613) 521-2457. According to Bradley, the company will consider civil or criminal action if warranted in the future.

Cal League Cards, P.O. Box 10031, Bakersfield, CA 93389

Inquiries of suspected counterfeit cards, or the sale thereof, should be addressed to company president Rick Smith at the address above. The minor league card manufacturer has not yet had problems in this area, but will consider prosecution of civil or criminal remedies if the situation arises.

Courtside Cards, 1247 Broadway Ave., Burlingame, CA 94010

Persons seeking authentication information may contact Stanley Chen at the above address. Reports of sales of suspected counterfeits should be directed to the attention of Tracy A. Chan. The company has not yet had to pursue action against counterfeiters, but would definitely do so in the future according to its president.

Action Packed, c/o LBC Sports, 851 N. Villa Ave., Villa Park, IL 60181

Persons with suspected counterfeit cards or information on persons selling such cards should contact William Rotz at the address above. No current counterfeits are known, but the company will consider action if counterfeits are found.

Upper Deck, 5909 Sea Otter Place, Carlsbad, CA 92008

While the hot-stamped hologram on the back of UD cards has proved an effective deterrent to counterfeiters, the company will authenticate any suspected cards if directed to the address above, to the attention of Ed Anderson, Director of Security. Persons with information about the sale of counterfeit/unauthorized product are asked to contact company president Richard McWilliam at that address. The company's director of marketing, Bruce Regis, said, "We have gone to great extremes to rid the hobby of counterfeiting and we would prosecute counterfeiters to the fullest extent of the law.

Skybox, c/o NBA Properties Inc., Olympic Tower, 645 Fifth Ave., New York, NY 10022

The licensor, NBA Properties, claims responsibility for investigation and acting on complaints of "all authorized merchandise bearing the trademarks of the NBA and/or its member teams, including trading cards." According to public relations director Chris Eckman, "NBAP is always watching the marketplace to uncover and prosecute counterfeiters." He commented, "It is truly a shame that a few disreputable printers and distributors are damaging a hobby enjoyed by millions of people." He indicated the company has undertaken investigations regarding counterfeits in the past and would do so in the future. Inquiries may be directed to the above address.

☆   ☆   ☆

The companies which did not respond to the survey were: Leaf-Donruss, Score, Topps, ProCards, Pro Set, Swell, Best Cards, Mothers Cookies, NBA Hoops, Classic Games, and Star Co.

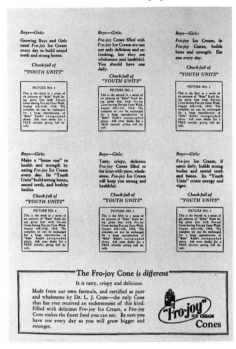

Our ability to present detailed analysis of "real" versus "fake" on this issue is hampered by a lack of known genuine examples to compare with known and/or suspected counterfeits.

Produced as part of a hard-sell campaign to get youngsters addicted to a particular brand of ice cream, surviving genuine Fro-joy baseball cards are rare and valuable today (single cards are worth up to $150 each). Even scarcer are genuine uncut sheets of the six Babe Ruth cards which comprise the set.

The same cannot be said for the counterfeit sheet, and single cards cut therefrom. Fake sheets are so prevalent, and

Counterfeit

George Herman ("Babe") Ruth

"The Sultan of Swat," who holds the world's record for home-run hits in a single season with 60 circuit clouts during the regular playing season of 1927, topped by 2 more against Pittsburgh during the World's Series games last year.

Counterfeit

Look Out, Mr. Pitcher!

This is the formidable picture the enemy slabman has to face. All of the "Babe's" bats have names. He made his 1926 record with "Black Betsy," a brunette, afterwards broken. The one in the picture is the King's current favorite, "Big Bertha," an ash blonde.

Counterfeit

genuine sheets are so rare, that all sheets encountered should be viewed with extreme suspicion until further data becomes available and can be published.

This particular counterfeit is often encountered in non-hobby settings such as flea markets. A wise course of action would be to avoid all such sheets and cards that are offered by non-hobby dealers and to seek a lifetime guarantee of authenticity for any specimens purchased within the hobby.

Several "generations" of counterfeit sheets are seen in the market. Not only have counterfeits been made from an original sheet, but counterfeits of the counterfeits have been made, with at least three different types known.

Recently a new type of Fro-joy counterfeit uncut sheet has been seen, overprinted with color tints. No genuine Fro-joy cards are known with color printing.

When The "Babe" Comes Home

Feet first, the "Babe" beats the ball to the home plate by inches. He doesn't have to do this often. Usually he "dog trots" around after a circuit smash. But when the occasion arises, the "Big Bat Boy", in spite of his bulk, can run bases with the best of them.

Counterfeit

"Babe" Ruth's Grip!

This is how "Babe" Ruth grips his bat as he steps up to add one more home run to his long string. Try it out on your own "Louisville Slugger."

Counterfeit

Ruth is a Crack Fielder

The Big Leagues cannot boast a surer fielder than the Home Run King. The photograph shows him scooping up a liner preparatory to a double play that retired the opposing team and put the game on ice for the World's Champions.

Counterfeit

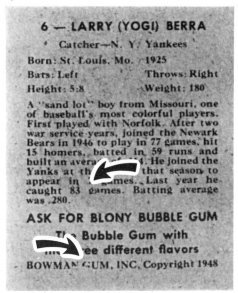

Black-and-white cards are much easier and cheaper to counterfeit than color cards. Ironically, it is much more difficult to identify and describe counterfeit characteristics on a black-and-white card, even though it is fairly easy to spot a fake.

Such is the case with the 1948 Bowman Yogi Berra card. In creating the reproduction, the counterfeiters created a photo that has a much larger black dot structure than a genuine card. This gives the picture a darker overall appearance and a ten-

Genuine   **Counterfeit**

dency toward a lack of fine detail. However, without a genuine '48 Berra card for comparison, these subjective observations are not useful in the detection of a counterfeit.

One feature seen on the counterfeit examined may or may not be diagnostic, as it may or may not appear on other copies. On the specimen photographed, there is a vertical hairline of black ink about ¼'' long running from the top-right border of the card into the photo. Under magnification, this appears to be a printing flaw, rather than a design problem. Obviously, if a suspect card features an identical ink line, it is a counterfeit. Just because a card may not exhibit such a line, however, does not make it genuine.

The best place to determine the status of a '48 Berra card is on the back. Because the counterfeiters photoreproduced black type from the gray cardboard background on an original card, the type on the fake is much lighter than normal. There are also two flaws in the back printing — areas where the bottoms of several contiguous letters are not printed. The most noticeable is the very bottom line of type, which on the counterfeit features incomplete letters "N" and "G" in "BOWMAN GUM". A similar flaw can be observed in the last complete line of the biography. The counterfeit lacks the bottom details of the letters "gam" in "games".

The counterfeit '48 Bowman Berra card is also considerably (about 25%) heavier than a genuine card.

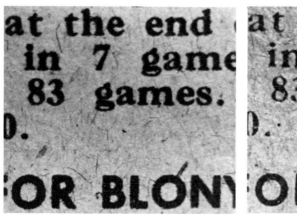 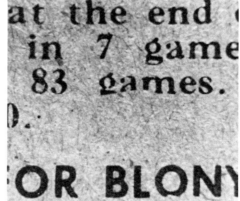

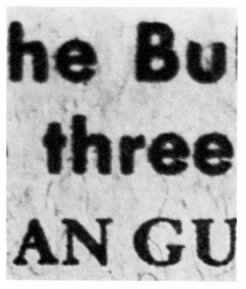 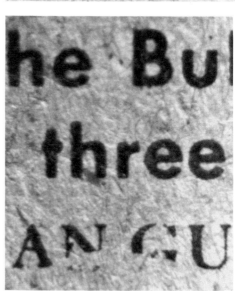

Genuine   **Counterfeit**

MICKEY MANTLE

Outfield—New York Yankees
Born: Commerce, Okla., Oct. 20, 1931
Height: 5-10   Weight: 175
Bats: Switch   Throws: Right

Mickey is the Yankee rookie of whom so much is expected in 1951. Everyone was talking about him during spring training in which he batted over .400. Kept on clicking when the regular season got under way. Spent most of the 1950 campaign with Joplin of the Western Association. In 137 games, hitting .383, and driving in 136 runs. Got 199 hits which included 30 doubles, 12 triples, 26 homers.

No. 253 in the 1951 SERIES

BASEBALL

PICTURE CARDS

©1951 Bowman Gum, Inc., Phila., Pa., U.S.A.

As this book went to press, no specimen of this counterfeit was available for examination. Photographs made some years back do not offer sufficient clarity of detail to allow a description of characteristics peculiar to this counterfeit.

The counterfeit lacks the clarity in the color printing on the front of a genuine card, and so is not particularly deceptive to a collector or dealer familiar with 1951 Bowmans.

No information about weight comparison between these counterfeits and the genuine Bowman cards is currently available.

No photo available

No photo available

Genuine   **Counterfeit**

MICKEY MANTLE

Outfield—New York Yankees
Born: Spavinaw, Okla., Oct. 20, 1931
Height: 5-11   Weight: 175
Bats: Switch   Throws: Right

Began the 1951 season with Yanks' Kansas City farm. Had batted in 50 runs in 40 games, and was sporting a .361 average, when called up by the parent club. In 96 games for the Bombers. Got 91 hits, including 13 home runs. Batted .267, and drove in 65 runs.

No. 101 in the 1952 SERIES

BASEBALL®

PICTURE CARDS

Get a $1.00 value Baseball Cap of your favorite major league team by sending 5 wrappers and 50 cents to BOWMAN Baseball, P. O. BOX 234, New York 23, N. Y. State size: small, medium or large.

© 1952 Bowman Gum Division, Haelan Laboratories, Inc., Phila. 44, Pa.—Ptd. in U. S. A.

As this book went to press, no specimen of this counterfeit was available for examination. Photographs made some years back do not offer sufficient clarity of detail to allow a description of characteristics peculiar to this counterfeit.

The counterfeit lacks the clarity in the color printing on the front of a genuine card, and so is not particularly deceptive to a collector or dealer familiar with 1952 Bowmans.

No information about weight comparison between these counterfeits and the genuine Bowman cards is currently available.

No photo available

No photo available

Genuine

Counterfeit

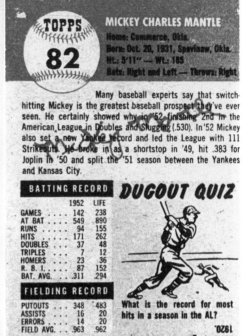

As this book went to press, no specimen of this counterfeit was available for examination. Photographs made some years back do not offer sufficient clarity of detail to allow a description of characteristics peculiar to this counterfeit.

The counterfeit lacks the clarity in the color printing on the front of a genuine card, and so is not particularly deceptive to a collector or dealer familiar with 1953 Topps.

No information about weight comparison between these counterfeits and the genuine Topps cards is currently available.

Genuine

Counterfeit

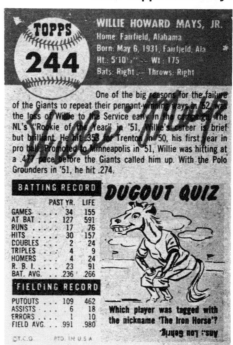

As this book went to press, no specimen of this counterfeit was available for examination. Photographs made some years back do not offer sufficient clarity of detail to allow a description of characteristics peculiar to this counterfeit.

The counterfeit lacks the clarity in the color printing on the front of a genuine card, and so is not particularly deceptive to a collector or dealer familiar with 1953 Topps.

No information about weight comparison between these counterfeits and the genuine Topps cards is currently available.

Genuine   **Counterfeit**

No photo available

No photo available

As this book went to press, no specimen or photograph of this counterfeit was available for examination.

By hobby standards an "old" counterfeit, having been produced in the early 1970s, this card is seldom seen today.

Only a single card from the '59 Fleer set was counterfeited, card #68, "Jan. 23, 1959 — Ted Signs for '59". Hobby lore has it that this card was pulled from distribution when Topps made a stink about its depiction of Red Sox general manager, who was still under baseball card contract with Topps. While most of the rest of the cards in this set sell for $3 in top grade, card #68 is a $450 card.

According to contemporary hobby press accounts, the counterfeit is easily spotted by the darkness of the printing on front and the extreme moire pattern on the front photo which resulted from a re-screening of a genuine card to make the counterfeit.

No photo available

No photo available

Genuine   **Counterfeit**

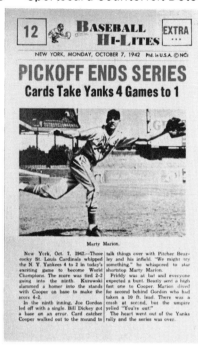

It has long been asserted in the hobby that this 72-card oversize (3¼x5⅜") set was counterfeited in its entirety back in the 1970s.

Reproducing the set would have been fairly easy since the fronts are printed in black-white-and-red, and the backs in black-white-and-green.

The allegation of counterfeiting is apparently based on the existence of cards which are much more poorly printed and detailed than others.

With no specimens of the alleged counterfeits to examine, at this point it is probably worth mentioning only as a cautionary note in the unlikely event that anyone would ever want to buy any of these cards.

Genuine   **Counterfeit**

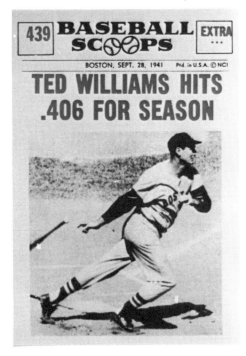

The entire run of this 80-card set is alleged to have been counterfeited in the 1970s.

Printed in black-white-and-red, it would not have been difficult to produce such counterfeits. One wonders, however, whether there could possibly have been a profit motivation since this set has never been popular with collectors. Even today, single cards in the set carry a largely optimistic book value of between 30¢ and $10 each, depending on which player is depicted in the particular great moment in baseball history.

The counterfeiting theory seems to be largely based on the appearance of cards which are much more poorly printed and detailed than others.

With inadequate specimens of the alleged counterfeits to examine, at this point it is probably worth mentioning only as a cautionary note in the unlikely event that anyone would ever want to buy any of these cards.

No photo available

No photo available

Genuine   **Counterfeit**

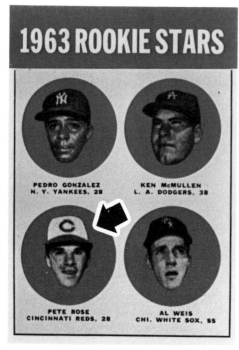

1963 ROOKIE STARS

PEDRO GONZALEZ
N. Y. YANKEES, 2B

KEN McMULLEN
L. A. DODGERS, 3B

PETE ROSE
CINCINNATI REDS, 2B

AL WEIS
CHI. WHITE SOX, SS

537	1963 ROOKIE STARS	MINOR LEAGUE LIFETIME RECORDS	G	AB	R	H	2B	3B	HR	RBI	AVG.
	PEDRO GONZALEZ N. Y. YANKEES—2B		595	2296	364	695	96	25	34	269	.304
	KEN McMULLEN L. A. DODGERS—3B		281	1022		96?	54		42	177	.285
	PETE ROSE CIN. REDS—2B		354	1345	301	427	59	52	12		.317
	AL WEIS CHI. WHITE SOX—SS		472	1870	314	497	59	18	15	159	.266

© T.C.G. PRINTED IN U.S.A.

(watermark: ORIGINAL REPRINT / COUNTERFEIT)

The first known counterfeit in modern baseball card history. According to contemporary press accounts, 10,000 of the fake '63 Rose cards were printed, but fewer than 200 were sold into the hobby before they were discovered and warnings issued.

The fake is easily distinguished by the naked eye through the appearance of a black outline around the Rose's white cap. No such outline appears on a genuine card. Conversely, the "C" on the cap, which should have a black outline, does not on the fake.

Printed on much thinner stock than a real '63 card, the printing from the other side of the counterfeit can be seen when the card is held to strong light. No light passes through a genuine '63 Topps card.

The court-ordered rubber-stamped blue "COUNTERFEIT" and red "ORIGINAL REPRINT" is found on most — but not all — of the counterfeits seen in today's market.

Genuine

Counterfeit

An overall fuzziness of the color printing on the front of this counterfeit, and an unnatural gloss to the front surface should raise warning flags.

Examination with a magnifying glass of the color design elements on the front of the card reveals sure evidence of the counterfeit's status.

Easy differentiation between real and fake on this card can be made by checking the red "1965 ROOKIE STARS" at the top of the card.

Those letters on a genuine card will be clean, solid red. On the counterfeit, these letters are composed of a pattern of tiny dots creating a fuzzy appearance at the edges. Similar dot structures can be seen at the edges of the players' names and positions. On back, the small black type is made fuzzy by an unintended red shadow of dots behind and left of the letters.

The black "Reprint" which appears on the back of the card shown here may not be present on all cards encountered in the hobby market.

Genuine

Counterfeit

PETE ROSE   2nd base

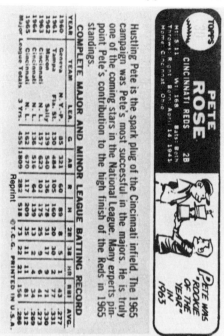

At first glance a pretty good imitation, an overall fuzziness of the color printing and an unnatural gloss to the front surface should raise suspicions.

Detailed examination of the color design elements reveals sure evidence of the counterfeit's status.

Easy differentiation between real and fake on this card can be made by checking the blue stripe and white "REDS" at the upper-left of the card.

Those letters on a genuine card will have clean edges. On the counterfeit, the edges of the letters are made fuzzy by a pattern of tiny blue dots creating a fuzzy appearance at the edges. A black hairline (literally) can be seen above and to the right of the "S" in "REDS" on the counterfeit. Likewise, the position, which should be rendered in solid black letters, is composed of tiny black dots.

The black "Reprint" which appears on the back of the card shown here may not be present on all cards encountered in the hobby market.

Genuine

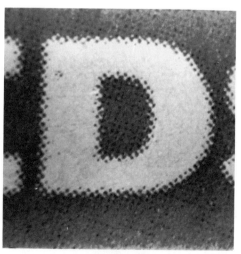

Counterfeit

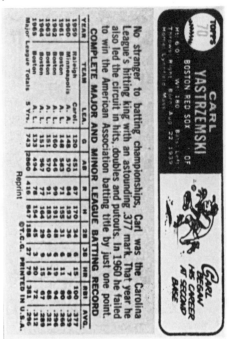

While an overall lack of crispness to the color printing and generally washed-out colors should raise warning flags when this card is viewed, such subjective indicators should not be relied upon in counterfeit card detection.

Using a magnifying glass to examine the lettering will provide definite proof that this card is a phony. On a genuine Topps card, the words "RED SOX" and the player's name and position will be printed as solid white (team and player name) or black (position) letters with edges that end crisply and cleanly at the red background bars. On this counterfeit, the edges of the letters are made fuzzy by a pattern of tiny blue and red dots.

On the back, the small black type which is made up of solid letters on the genuine card is seen as composed of tiny dots on the counterfeit.

The black "Reprint" which appears on the back of the card shown here may not be present on all cards encountered in the hobby market.

Genuine

Counterfeit

JIM PALMER   pitcher

A fairly good reproduction of the photo on a genuine Palmer rookie card may be misleading at first exposure to this counterfeit. When viewed outside of a card holder, however, the card exhibits an unnatural gloss on the front and a fuzziness of the black lettering.

Using a magnifying glass to examine the lettering, it will be found to provide definite proof that this card is a phony. On a genuine Topps card, the words "ORI-OLES", "JIM PALMER" and "pitcher" will be printed as solid black letters, with edges that end crisply and cleanly at the green background bars. On this counterfeit, the edges of the letters are made fuzzy by a pattern of tiny black dots which make up the letters.

It's interesting to note that all specimens of this counterfeit seen to date have no white border at the bottom of the card.

The black "Reprint" which appears on the back of the card shown here may not be present on all cards encountered.

Genuine

Counterfeit

Visually almost perfect, this counterfeit is often presented in a heavy plastic holder, disguising its weight of nearly 30% more than a genuine '67 Topps card.

The first visual clue a prospective buyer might have is on the card's back, where most of the counterfeits seen are too white. A genuine 25-year-old Topps card has usually yellowed somewhat. Since that, too, can be faked, the degree of aging evident on the back should not be used as a definitive indicator of status.

Rather, with a good magnifying glass, examine the signatures on the front. A genuine card will show these facsimile autographs as solid black letters. On the counterfeit, the letters of these signatures can be seen to have a "shadow" of tiny color dots visible beneath the black. This requires strong magnification to see, but on a card that sells for this much money, it's important to be sure.

The "COUNTERFEIT" stamp on the back of the photographed card is unique to that specimen.

Genuine   **Counterfeit**

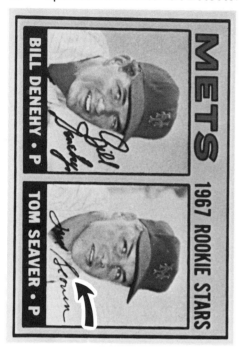

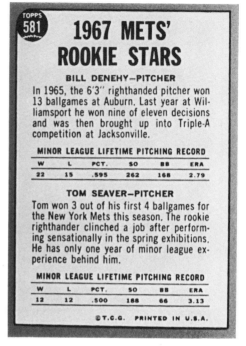

Visually almost perfect, this counterfeit is usually presented in a heavy plastic holder to disguise the fact that it weighs nearly 22% more than a genuine '67 Topps card.

The first visual clue a prospective buyer might have is on the card's back, where most of the counterfeits seen are too white. A genuine 25-year-old Topps card has usually yellowed somewhat. Since that, too, can be faked, the degree of age-ing evident on the back should not be used as a definitive indicator of genuine-ness status.

Rather, with a good magnifying glass, examine the areas of the signatures on the front. A genuine card will show these facsimile autographs as solid black letters. On the counterfeit, the letters of these signatures can be seen to have a "shadow" of tiny color dots visible beneath the black. This requires strong magnification to see, but on a card that sells for this much money, it's important to be sure.

Genuine

Counterfeit

No photo available

No photo available

Perhaps it would be better not to cast suspicions on all the genuine examples of this card without the "proof" of existence of a counterfeit version. However, we believe it is in the best interest of the hobby to err on the side of protection, and so will report the long-standing hobby rumor that a counterfeit '67 Brooks Robinson card exists, possibly created by the same hand as the fake Carew and Seaver rookies.

If such is the case, expect the fake Robby to be similarly deceptive and look for the same type of indicators of genuineness status as presented for the other two known counterfeit '67 Topps cards.

No photo available

No photo available

Genuine   **Counterfeit**

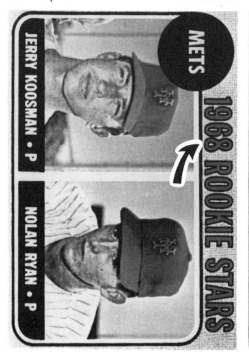

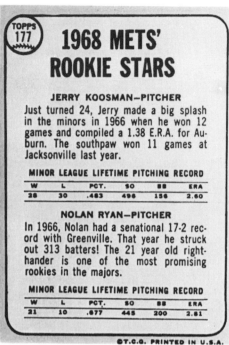

The counterfeit Nolan Ryan rookie card is easily identified by the existence of a dot pattern in the red letters and black outlines of "1968 ROOKIE STARS" at the top of the card. The genuine card has these letters in solid red, outlined with solid black.

Most people would describe the color of the fake card's back as more orange and less bright than on a genuine card, though it must be noted that there are wide color variances on the backs of genuine 1968 Topps baseball cards.

It appears that an attempt was made to mute and "age" the white cardboard of the counterfeit's back by brushing on a weak wash, perhaps watercolor or coffee.

Genuine

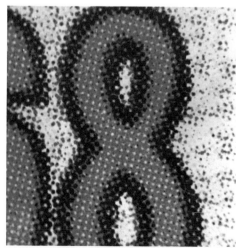

Counterfeit

A slightly glossy finish to the card and an overall fuzziness to the photo should alert a person who has any familiarity with genuine 1969 Topps baseball cards.

The definite indicators of this card's counterfeit status will be found in the magenta circle at the upper-left. On a genuine card, each element — the black perimeter of the circle, the black and white name, the black "Outfield" and the magenta background — will be printed in solid color. The counterfeit exhibits these elements as a composition of tiny dots, totally unlike the crisp, clean elements of the genuine card. Similar fuzziness will be noted on the counterfeit in the black outlines of the team name letters at bottom.

Most viewers would describe the background color of the card's back as being more orange than the genuine '69 Topps cards, which are something of a salmon color. The word "REPRINT" which appears on the back of the card shown here may not be present on all specimens of this counterfeit.

Genuine   **Counterfeit**

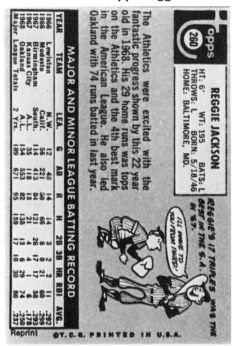

Many hobbyists, upon viewing this counterfeit for the first time may think they've lucked onto an unusually well-centered specimen of the Reggie rookie card. However, a slightly glossy finish on the front and an overall fuzziness to the photo should raise a warning flag to a person who has a passing familiarity with genuine 1969 Topps baseball cards.

While definite indicators of this card's counterfeit status can be found in the purple circle at the upper-right (a fuzziness of elements that should be printed in solid colors), it is easier to present in a black-and-white photograph the differences to be found in the letters of "ATHLETICS" at the bottom of the card.

The counterfeit exhibits the black lines around the yellow letters as a series of tiny black dots, totally unlike the solid black lines found on the genuine card.

The word "REPRINT", which appears on the back of the card shown here may not be present on all specimens of this counterfeit.

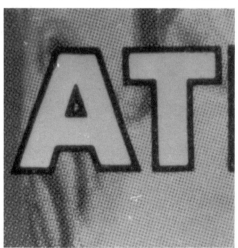

Genuine

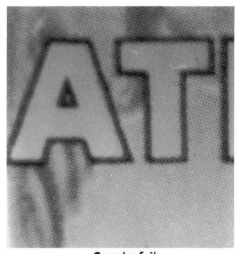

Counterfeit

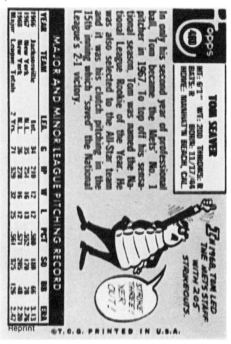

A slightly glossy finish on the front and an overall fuzziness to the photo should raise a warning flag to a person who has a passing familiarity with genuine 1969 Topps baseball cards.

While definite indicators of this card's counterfeit status can be found in the purple circle at the upper-right (a fuzziness of elements that should be printed in solid colors), it is easier to present in a black-and-white photograph the differences to be found in the letters of "METS" at the bottom of the card.

The counterfeit exhibits the black lines around the yellow letters as a series of tiny black dots, totally unlike the solid black lines found on the genuine card.

Most viewers would describe the background color of the card's back as being more orange in tone than the genuine '69 Topps cards, which are more of a salmon color. The word "REPRINT", which appears on the back of the card shown here may not be present on all specimens of this counterfeit.

Genuine

Counterfeit

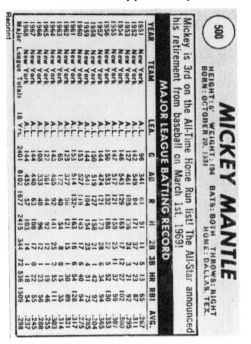

A slightly glossy finish to the card and an overall fuzziness to the photo should raise the suspicions of a person who has some familiarity with genuine 1969 Topps baseball cards. As with most counterfeit cards, however, it will take a magnifying lens to make a final determination.

The easiest identifiers are to be found in the red circle at the front upper-left, containing the player's name and position. On a genuine card, each element — the black perimeter of the circle, the white and yellow name, the black "1st Base" and the red background — will be printed in solid color. The counterfeit exhibits these elements in a composition of tiny dots, totally unlike the crisp, clean elements of the genuine card. Similar fuzziness will be noted on the counterfeit in the black outlines of the team name letters at bottom.

The word "REPRINT", which appears on the back of the card shown here may not be present on all specimens of this counterfeit.

Genuine

Counterfeit

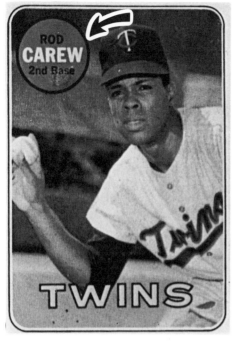

YEAR	TEAM	LEA.	G	AB	R	H	2B	3B	HR	RBI	AVG.
1964	Melbourne Tw.	Fla. Rk.	37	123	17	40	5	3	0	21	.325
1965	Orlando	Fla. St.	125	439	57	133	20	8	1	52	.303
1966	Wilson	Carol.	112	383	64	112	19	2	1	30	.292
1967	Minnesota	A.L.	137	514	66	150	22	7	8	51	.292
1968	Minnesota	A.L.	127	461	46	126	27	2	1	42	.273
	Major League Totals 2 Yrs.	A.L.	264	975	112	276	49	9	9	93	.283

MAJOR AND MINOR LEAGUE BATTING RECORD

One of the leading batters in the A.L., Rod finished eleventh in the circuit in batting last season. As late as August 22nd, the second baseman was leading the American League in hitting. Rod's favorite club in 1968 was the World Champion Tigers . . . He blasted Detroit pitching for a .444 clip last season.

Topps 510

ROD CAREW
HT: 6' WT: 170 BATS: L
THROWS: R BORN: 10/1/45
HOME: BROOKLYN, N.Y.

ROD HAS BEEN THE ALL-STAR 2nd BASE-MAN TWICE.

'67 '68

Reprint   ©T.C.G. PRINTED IN U.S.A.

A quick glance at the blue circle containing the player's name and position will identify this counterfeit. A printing flaw under the word "Base" has created a mess of black and white violations in the blue background. A slightly glossy finish to the card and an overall fuzziness to the photo should also raise the suspicions of persons familiar with genuine 1969 Topps baseball cards.

Other definite identifiers are to be found in the blue circle. On a genuine card, each element — the black perime-ter of the circle, the black and white name, the black "2nd Base" and the blue background — will be printed in solid color. The counterfeit exhibits these elements in a composition of tiny dots, totally unlike the crisp, clean elements of the genuine card. Similar fuzziness will be noted on the counterfeit in the black outlines of the team name letters at bottom.

The word "REPRINT", which appears on the back of the card shown here may not be present on all specimens.

Genuine

Counterfeit

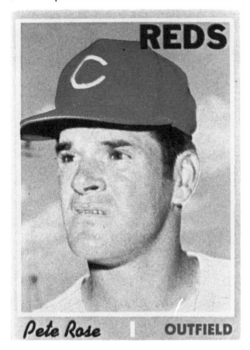

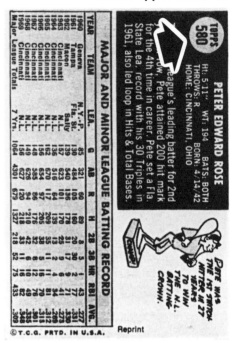

An overall fuzziness of the color printing on the front of this counterfeit should raise warning flags. Close examination of the team name and the player's name reveals even more fuzziness at the edges than will be seen on a genuine card.

However, easiest differentiation between real and fake on this card can be made by checking the area of the card number on the back of the card.

On a genuine card, the "TOPPS" and "580" will be clean, solid blue and the background circle will be pure yellow. On the counterfeit, a pattern of tiny blue dots intrudes into the yellow circle, while the blue letters will be littered with yellow dots. Likewise, the rest of the back printing, including the blue printed stats and the cartoon, are composed of dots on the counterfeit, rather than being solid as on a Topps original.

The black "Reprint" which appears on the back of the card shown here may not be present on all cards encountered in the hobby market.

Genuine

Counterfeit

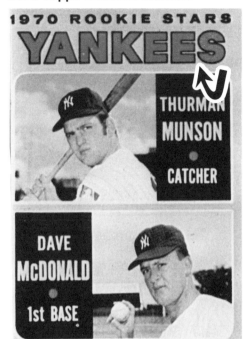

An unnatural glossiness on the front of the card and overall fuzziness of printing on both sides makes this counterfeit fairly easy to spot.

Examination of the color design details with a magnifying glass reveals sure evidence of the counterfeit's status.

Easy differentiation between real and fake on this card can be made by examining the large red "YANKEES" on the front of the card.

Those letters on a genuine card will be clean, solid red, with solid black outlines.

On the counterfeit, the letters are composed of many tiny dots, giving a fuzzy appearance. Similar evidence can be seen in the letters of "1970 ROOKIE STARS" and in the players' names and positions.

On back, the blue printed wording is likewise composed of dots, rather than being solid as on a Topps original.

The black "Reprint" which appears on the back of the card shown here may not be present on all cards encountered in the hobby market.

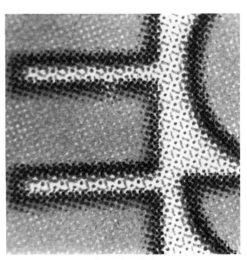

Genuine   **Counterfeit**

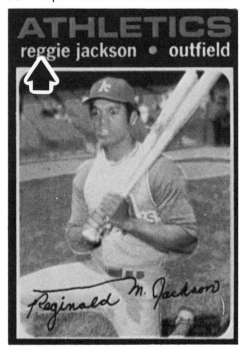

Not a particularly deceptive counterfeit, this card displays an overall lack of sharpness in the photo and front color design elements.

With the use of a magnifying glass, the cause of that fuzziness can be used to pinpoint the status of this card as counterfeit. Close examination of the red-orange "ATHLETICS" and the yellow player name at the top of the card will reveal on the counterfeit that the letters are comprised of many tiny color dots, rather than the sharp, clean lines of the letters on a genuine card.

Similarly, the facsimile autograph, which on a genuine card is comprised of sharp black lines, is reproduced on the counterfeit as a collection of black dots.

Genuine

Counterfeit

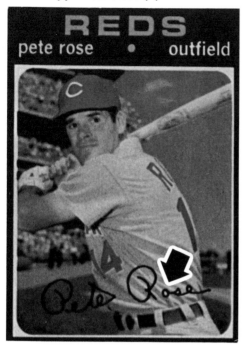

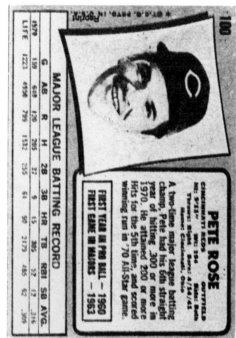

Because of the color combination of the player and team name and position at the top of the card, this counterfeit is not as easy to spot as the other known 1971 Topps counterfeits.

Still, a quick glance with a magnifying glass at the area of the facsimile signature will tell good from bad. A genuine '71 Topps Pete Rose card will have the autograph reproduced as a solid black element. On the counterfeit, the signature is composed of many tiny black dots, giving it a fuzzy appearance.

Genuine

Counterfeit

No photo available

No photo available

No specimen has yet been made available for examination and photography.

According to a May 15, 1983, article in *Baseball Card News*, this card is one of a group of eight 1971-1973 Topps baseball cards that were apparently produced by the same hand. The fakes surfaced in Southern California but then, as now, were rarely seen in the hobby market.

Unlike virtually every other counterfeit, the persons responsible for production of this group did not simply photo-reproduce the existing typography on the genuine cards, but rather had most of it — front and back — reset. The noticeable differences in size and shape of type which resulted make this group of counterfeits fairly easy to spot.

An even more noticeable difference between the cards in this group and genuine Topps cards is that (with the exception of the 1973 Schmidt rookie) all of the fakes have omitted the Topps copyright symbol (©) before the copyright line on the back of the card.

No photo available

No photo available

Genuine   **Counterfeit**

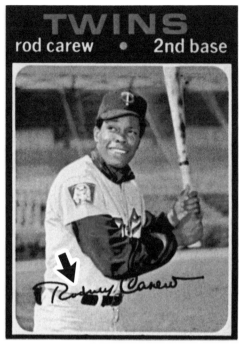

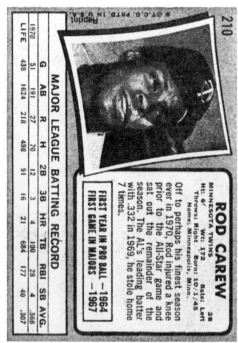

Not a particularly deceptive counterfeit, this card displays an overall lack of sharpness in the photo and front color design elements.

Because of the color scheme used on this particular card for the team and player names and the position, it is easier to spot this counterfeit by examination of the black facsimile autograph.

On a genuine card, the signature is comprised of sharp black lines. The counterfeit reproduces the autograph as a collection of black dots, creating a fuzzy appearance.

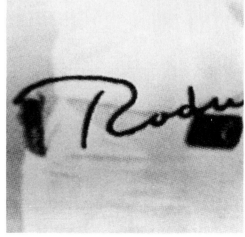

Genuine   **Counterfeit**

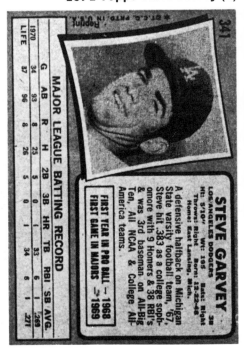

Not a particularly deceptive counterfeit, this card displays an overall lack of sharpness in the photo and front color design elements.

With the use of a magnifying glass, the cause of that fuzziness can be used to pinpoint the status of this card as counterfeit. Close examination of the red-orange "DODGERS", the orange player name and the yellow position at the top of the card will reveal on the counterfeit that the letters are comprised of many tiny color dots, rather than the sharp, clean lines of the letters on a genuine card.

Similarly, the facsimile autograph, which on a genuine card is comprised of sharp black lines, is reproduced on the counterfeit as a collection of black dots.

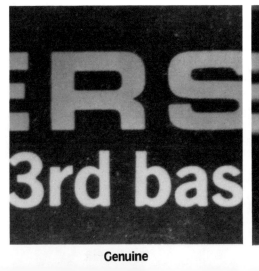

Genuine

Counterfeit

No photo available

No photo available

No specimen has yet been made available for examination and photography.

According to a May 15, 1983, article in *Baseball Card News*, this card is one of a group of eight 1971-1973 Topps baseball cards that were apparently produced by the same hand. The fakes surfaced in Southern California but then, as now, were rarely seen in the hobby market.

Unlike virtually every other counterfeit, the persons responsible for production of this group did not simply photo-reproduce the existing typography on the genuine cards, but rather had most of it — front and back — reset. The noticeable differences in size and shape of type which resulted make this group of counterfeits fairly easy to spot.

An even more noticeable difference between the cards in this group and genuine Topps cards is that (with the exception of the 1973 Schmidt rookie) all of the fakes have omitted the Topps copyright line on the back of the card.

No photo available

No photo available

Genuine   **Counterfeit**

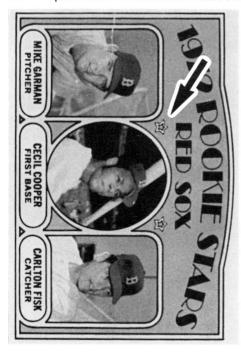

An overall fuzzy appearance on the front makes this counterfeit look suspicious to an experienced eye.

Examination of the design details with a magnifying glass reveals sure evidence of the counterfeit's status.

Easy differentiation between real and fake on this card can be made by examining the stars above the photo of Cecil Cooper. On a genuine card, the stars will be outlined in clean, solid black. On the counterfeit, the black lines are composed of tiny dots, giving a fuzzy appearance. Similar evidence can be seen in the other black framelines and all of the lettering on the front of the counterfeit.

On the back, a black printed screen has been used to simulate the gray cardboard of a Topps original and hide the white cardboard on which the fake was printed.

The black ''Reprint'' which appears on the back of the card shown here may not be present on all cards encountered in the hobby market.

Genuine

Counterfeit

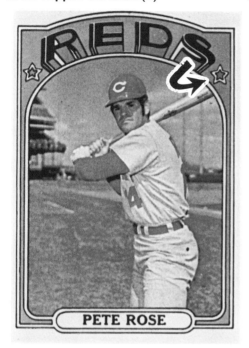

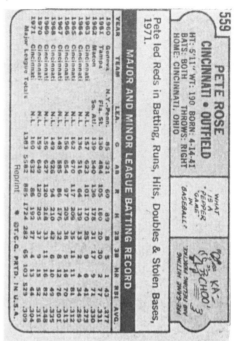

Because it is printed on thinner, whiter cardboard than the genuine 1972 Topps cards, and because the gloss of the card's front differs from that on a genuine card, an experienced dealer or collector should be able to spot this counterfeit with relative ease.

The presence of dot structures where they should not be provides evidence against the counterfeit, but does require a magnifying glass to verify.

The player's name, the black pinstripes and the stars to either side of "REDS" are the best places to examine a suspect card. On a genuine card, these elements will appear as clean, solid black lines. The counterfeit shows these elements as being made up of many tiny dots.

Similarly, the black letters on the counterfeit's back are of fuzzy composition.

The black "Reprint" which appears on the back of the card photographed here may not be present on all cards encountered in the hobby market.

Genuine

Counterfeit

No photo available

No photo available

No specimen has yet been made available for examination and photography.

According to a May 15, 1983, article in *Baseball Card News*, this card is one of a group of eight 1971-1973 Topps baseball cards that were apparently produced by the same hand. The fakes surfaced in Southern California but then, as now, were rarely seen in the hobby market.

Unlike virtually every other counterfeit, the persons responsible for production of this group did not simply photo-reproduce the existing typography on the genuine cards, but rather had most of it — front and back — reset. The noticeable differences in size and shape of type which resulted make this group of counterfeits fairly easy to spot.

An even more noticeable difference between the cards in this group and genuine Topps cards is that (with the exception of the 1973 Schmidt rookie) all of the fakes have omitted the Topps copyright symbol (©) before the copyright line on the back of the card.

No photo available

No photo available

Genuine

Counterfeit

No photo available

No photo available

No specimen has yet been made available for examination and photography.

According to a May 15, 1983, article in *Baseball Card News*, this card is one of a group of eight 1971-1973 Topps baseball cards that were apparently produced by the same hand. The fakes surfaced in Southern California but then, as now, were rarely seen in the hobby market.

Unlike virtually every other counterfeit, the persons responsible for production of this group did not simply photo-reproduce the existing typography on the genuine cards, but rather had most of it — front and back — reset. The noticeable differences in size and shape of type which resulted make this group of counterfeits fairly easy to spot.

An even more noticeable difference between the cards in this group and genuine Topps cards is that (with the exception of the 1973 Schmidt rookie) all of the fakes have omitted the Topps copyright symbol (©) before the copyright line on the back of the card.

No photo available

No photo available

Genuine   **Counterfeit**

No photo available

No photo available

No specimen has yet been made available for examination and photography.

According to a May 15, 1983, article in *Baseball Card News*, this card is one of a group of eight 1971-1973 Topps baseball cards that were apparently produced by the same hand. The fakes surfaced in Southern California but then, as now, were rarely seen in the hobby market.

Unlike virtually every other counterfeit, the persons responsible for production of this group did not simply photo-reproduce the existing typography on the genuine cards, but rather had most of it — front and back — reset. The noticeable differences in size and shape of type which resulted make this group of counterfeits fairly easy to spot.

An even more noticeable difference between the cards in this group and genuine Topps cards is that (with the exception of the 1973 Schmidt rookie) all of the fakes have omitted the Topps copyright symbol (©) before the copyright line on the back of the card.

No photo available

No photo available

Genuine

Counterfeit

HANK
AARON
ATLANTA BRAVES   **1st BASE**

According to a May 15, 1983, article in *Baseball Card News*, this card is one of a group of eight 1971-1973 Topps baseball card) that were apparently produced by the same hand. The fakes surfaced in Southern California but then, as now, were rarely seen in the hobby market.

Unlike virtually every other counterfeit, the persons responsible for production of this group did not simply photo-reproduce the existing typography on the genuine cards, but rather had most of it — front and back — reset. The noticeable differences in size and shape of type which resulted make this group of counterfeits fairly easy to spot. The stats on back of the counterfeit, for example, are much smaller than on a genuine card.

An even more noticeable difference between the cards in this group and genuine Topps cards is that (with the exception of the 1973 Schmidt rookie) all of the fakes have omitted the Topps copyright symbol (©) before the copyright line on the back of the card.

Genuine   **Counterfeit**

The fuzzy photo and lettering on the front of this counterfeit should put most hobbyists on notice that more detailed examination is needed.

Using a magnifying glass to examine the lettering will provide definite proof that this card is a phony. On a genuine card, such details as the player and team names and position should appear as solid letters with edges that end crisply and cleanly at the white background. On this counterfeit, the letters are composed of

many tiny color dots, giving them a ragged look at the edges. The back is likewise not very deceptive. The black lettering is fuzzy and close examination will show a pattern of black and yellow dots has been printed on the white cardboard to simulate the genuine Topps card stock.

The black "Reprint" which appears on the back of the card shown here may not be present on all cards offered for prospective purchase.

Genuine

Counterfeit

WILLIE
MAYS ←   OUTFIELD

This card is one of a group of eight 1971-1973 Topps baseball cards that surfaced in Southern California around 1982.

Unlike virtually every other counterfeit, the persons responsible for production of this group did not simply photo-reproduce the existing typography on the genuine cards, but rather had most of it — front and back — reset. The noticeable differences in size and shape of type which resulted make this group of counterfeits fairly easy to spot.

This counterfeit Mays card is the easiest of the group to identify because the counterfeits forgot to include the team name at the lower left corner of the card's front.

On the back, the counterfeit exhibits much smaller type in the statistics than on a genuine card. The copyright symbol (©) is also missing from the fake. On a genuine card, it will appear before the copyright line at the bottom of the card's back.

Genuine

Counterfeit

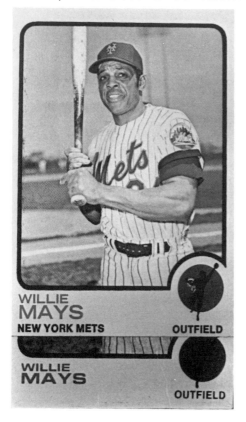

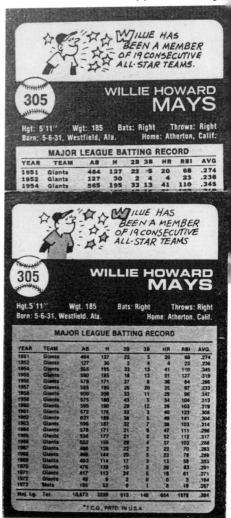

The counterfeiter of a group of early 1970s Topps star cards took the unusual step of resetting the type on the front and back of the cards, in styles and sizes slightly different from the genuine cards. Note on the front of the Willie Mays counterfeit (bottom left), the team name was omitted. The stats on the back of the counterfeit (bottom right) are much smaller than on the original.

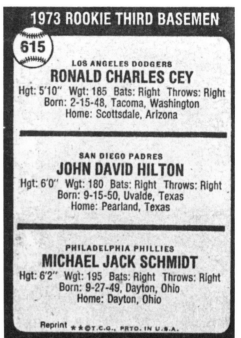

An overall fuzzy appearance of the player photos and front lettering makes this counterfeit look suspicious at first glance. Examination of the design details with a magnifying glass reveals sure evidence of the counterfeit's status.

Easy differentiation between real and fake on this card can be made by examining the player and team names. Those letters on a genuine card will be clean, solid blue (name) or black (team) letters. On the counterfeit, they are composed of many dots, giving a fuzzy appearance.

Similar evidence can be seen in the black frames around the player's photos and in "1973 ROOKIE THIRD BASEMEN" at top.

On back, a black and yellow dot pattern has been printed to simulate the cardboard of a Topps original and hide the white cardboard on which the fake was printed.

The black "Reprint" which appears on the back of the card shown here may not be present on all cards encountered in the hobby market.

Genuine

Counterfeit

No photo available

No photo available

No specimen has yet been made available for examination and photography.

According to a May 15, 1983, article in *Baseball Card News*, this card is one of a group of eight 1971-1973 Topps baseball cards that were apparently produced by the same hand. The fakes surfaced in Southern California but then, as now, were rarely seen in the hobby market.

Unlike virtually every other counterfeit, the persons responsible for production of this group did not simply photo-reproduce the existing typography on the genuine cards, but rather had most of it — front and back — reset. The noticeable differences in size and shape of type which resulted make this group of counterfeits fairly easy to spot.

An even more noticeable difference between the cards in this group and genuine Topps cards is that (with the exception of this 1973 Schmidt rookie) all of the fakes have omitted the Topps copyright symbol (©) before the copyright line on the back of the card.

No photo available

No photo available

Genuine

Counterfeit

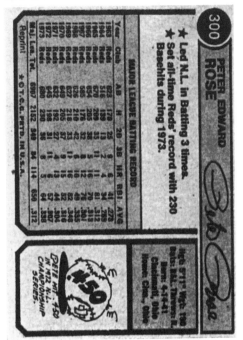

The fuzzy photo and lettering on the front of this counterfeit should put most hobbyists on notice that more detailed examination is needed.

Using a magnifying glass to examine the lettering will provide definite proof that this card is a phony. On a genuine card, such details as the black borders of the orange frame line, the player's name, team and position and the red banners should appear as solid colors with edges that end crisply and cleanly at the respective backgrounds. On this counterfeit, the letters and other color design elements are composed of many tiny color dots, giving them a ragged look at the edges. The back is likewise not very deceptive. The black lettering is fuzzy and close examination shows a pattern of black dots printed on the white cardboard to simulate the genuine Topps card stock.

The black "Reprint" which appears on the back of the card shown here may not be present on all cards offered for prospective purchase.

Genuine

Counterfeit

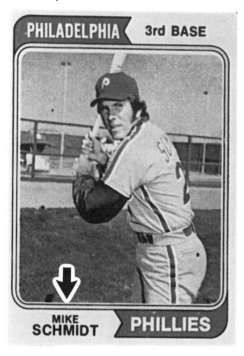

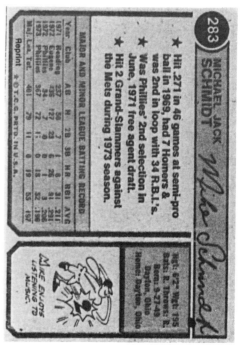

An overall fuzziness of appearance on the front of this counterfeit was created by the re-screening of design elements to create printing materials for the counterfeit.

The result is that elements that should be composed of solid black letters and lines have been reproduced on the counterfeit as a composite of tiny color dots. This is especially noticeable in the black frame lines around the photo and team name flags, and in the player's name and position.

Genuine

Counterfeit

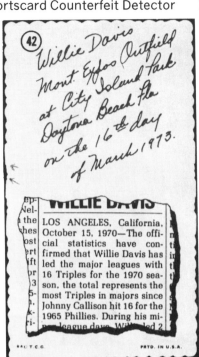

Original cards of this test issue are so scarce that most hobbyists have never seen one. It should be assumed that each of the 72 large-format (2⅞x5'') cards in the issue was counterfeited, though not all have been seen to date.

Generally, the counterfeits can be seen to have a much grayer appearance than the genuine black-and-white cards, lacking much of the contrast. This is caused by the counterfeit having a black dot structure to the photo that is much heavier than the genuine.

The easiest method of distinguishing the counterfeit '74 deckles from the genuine cards is to examine the area of the blue facsimile signature on the front of the card. The counterfeits have a black "shadow" of dots visible under magnification beneath the signature. This is not present on genuine cards.

The word "Fake" which was penned on the front of the card shown here will not be present on cards encountered in the hobby market.

Genuine

Counterfeit

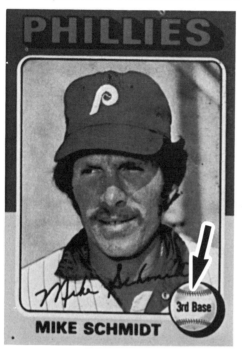

While the player photo on this counterfeit is fairly deceptive, many hobbyists would be immediately suspicious of the card based on a general fuzziness of the other color elements on the front, especially in the areas of black printing.

Such things as the frame around the photo, the player's name, facsimile autograph and position should be represented as clean, solid lines. On the counterfeit, these elements are composed of many tiny black dots.

Easy differentiation between real and fake card can be made by examining the ''3rd Base'' inside the ball at lower right.

The card back also lacks any contrast, the result of red and green ink being used to simulate the gray cardboard of a genuine Topps card and hide the white cardboard on which the counterfeit was produced.

The black ''Reprint'' which appears on the back of the card shown here may not be present on all cards encountered in the hobby market.

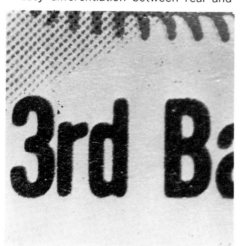

Genuine   **Counterfeit**

Hobbyists who are familiar with the genuine Brett rookie card might be immediately suspicious of this counterfeit based on a generally poor ability to mimic the colors of the genuine card, especially in the area of the team name. Overall, the colors on front of the fake are not as bold as on the real thing. However, as the perception of color is subjective among individuals, and because even genuine cards can vary widely in the intensity or shade of color, it is never recommended to base an authenticity judgement on color alone.

Easy differentiation between real and fake on this card can be made by examining the "3rd Base" inside the ball at lower right. Those letters on a genuine card will be clean, solid black; on the counterfeit, they are composed of many dots, giving a fuzzy appearance.

The black "Reprint" which appears on the back of the card shown here may not be present on all cards encountered in the hobby market.

Genuine

Counterfeit

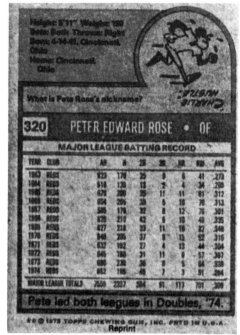

Because it is printed on thinner, whiter cardboard than genuine 1975 Topps cards, and the gloss of the card's front differs from that on a genuine card, an experienced hobbyist should be able to easily spot this counterfeit.

The presence of dot structures where they should not be is evidence of the counterfeit, but requires a magnifying glass to verify. The "NL ALL STAR" designation and position in the star at lower right are the best places to examine a sus-pect card. On a genuine card, these words will appear as clean, solid magenta ("NL ALL STAR") or black ("Outfield") letters. The counterfeit shows these elements as being made up of many tiny dots.

The counterfeit's back lacks contrast because red and green ink was used to simulate the gray background.

The black "Reprint" which appears on the back of the card photographed here may not be present on all cards encoun-tered in the hobby market.

Genuine

Counterfeit

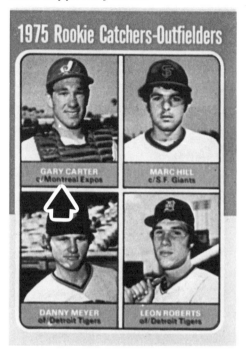

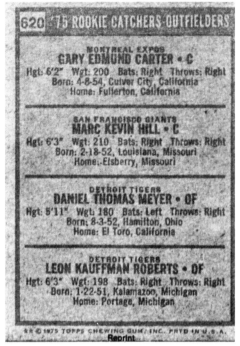

Because it is printed on thinner, whiter cardboard than the genuine 1975 Topps cards, and because the gloss on the front differs from that on a genuine card, an experienced hobbyist should be able to spot this counterfeit with relative ease.

The presence of dot structures where they should not be provides evidence against the counterfeit, but does require a magnifying glass to verify.

The players' names and teams are the best places to examine a suspect card. On a genuine card, these words will appear as clean, solid white (names) or black (teams) letters. The counterfeit shows these elements as being made up of many tiny dots.

Red and green ink used on the back to simulate gray cardboard gives the counterfeit's reverse a muddy appearance.

The black "Reprint" which appears on the back of the card photographed here may not be present on all cards encountered in the hobby market.

Genuine

Counterfeit

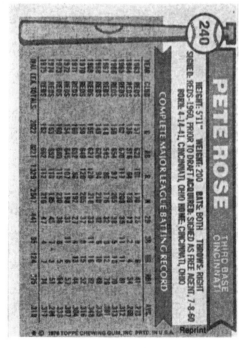

While the player's photo on this counterfeit is quite deceptive, the fact that all of the other front design elements were re-screened from an original card makes this counterfeit fairly easy to identify — as long as a magnifying glass is at hand.

A quick check of the star at lower-left provides the proof of status. A genuine card will have the "NL ALL STAR" in crisp, clean green letters, and the position in solid black letters. The counterfeit shows these elements as being made up of many tiny dots.

The green printing on the back has little of the original card's contrast, as a result of being printed over a screened black pattern designed to make the thin white cardboard stock of the fake look like the traditional gray Topps cardstock.

The black "Reprint" which appears on the back of the card shown here may not be present on all cards encountered in buy and sell transactions.

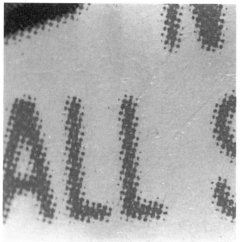

Genuine   **Counterfeit**

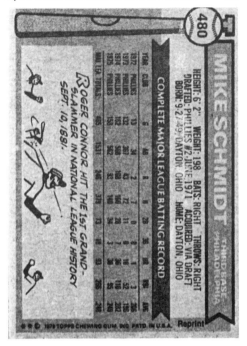

Because it is printed on thinner, whiter cardboard than the genuine 1976 Topps cards, and because the gloss of the card's front differs from that on a genuine card, an experienced dealer or collector should be able to spot this counterfeit with relative ease.

A fuzzy-appearing player photo and the fact that all of the other front design elements were re-screened from an original card make this counterfeit easy to identify — as long as a magnifying glass is at hand.

A quick check of the color bars at the bottom of the card provides the proof of status. A genuine card will have the yellow and magenta stripes printed in solid colors. The player's name on a genuine card will be printed in solid black letters. The counterfeit shows these elements as being made up of many tiny dots.

The black "Reprint" which appears on the back of the card shown here may not be present on all cards encountered in buy and sell transactions.

Genuine   **Counterfeit**

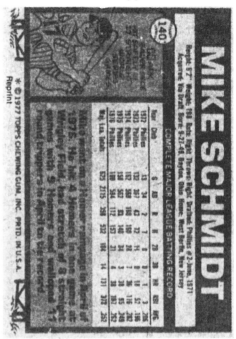

Not particularly deceptive because of an unusual gloss on the front and an overall fuzziness of the color printing, this counterfeit is easily identifiable using a magnifying glass. The proof of this counterfeit's status can be easily seen at the top-front of the card. There, the black outlines of the team name, the green rendering of the player's name, and the black printing in and around the yellow flag can be seen on the counterfeit to be made up of many small color dots. On a genuine card, these elements will be solid color, with no discernible dot pattern.

While you have your glass out, check the gray background on the back of the card. Note that it has been produced by printing a screened black pattern onto otherwise white cardboard. The thinner-than-genuine white cardboard stock can be seen on the edges of the card.

The black "Reprint" which appears on the back of the specimen photographed here may not be present on all cards encountered in the market.

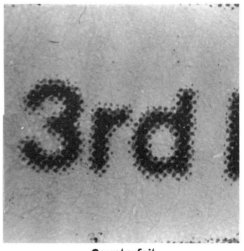

Genuine   **Counterfeit**

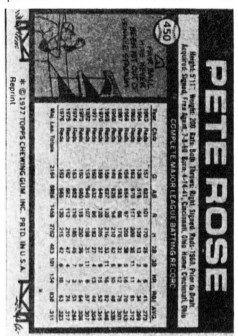

The use of a magnifying glass to check virtually any of the non-photo color elements on the front of this counterfeit will immediately and irrefutably brand the fake. The black printing, such as the frame lines around the photo and team name, the player's name and the shadow under the flag are seen as composed of many tiny dots, rather than as clean black lines and letters as found on an original card.

The counterfeit's back lacks the contrast of an original as a result of the green ink being printed over a screened black pattern designed to make the thin white cardboard stock of the fake look like the traditional gray Topps cardstock.

The black "Reprint" which appears on the back of the specimen photographed here may not be present on all cards encountered in buy and sell transactions.

Genuine

Counterfeit

A definite fuzziness of the color printing on the front, along with an unnatural gloss, combine with back printing almost totally lacking contrast to produce this rather easy-to-spot counterfeit.

As always, however, get out the magnifying glass to be sure. An examination of Andre Dawson's name and team are all that is necessary to brand this card a fake. On a genuine Dawson rookie, his name should appear in solid black letters, and his team name in solid magenta let-

ters. The counterfeit renders these words as a composite of tiny color dots.

The counterfeit's back lacks the contrast of an original as a result of the green ink being printed over a screened black pattern designed to make the thin white cardboard stock of the fake look like the traditional gray Topps cardstock.

The black "Reprint" which appears on the back of the specimen photographed here may not be present on all cards encountered in buy and sell transactions.

Genuine   **Counterfeit**

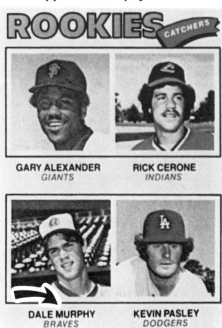

A definite fuzziness of the color printing on the front, along with an unnatural gloss, combine with back printing almost totally lacking contrast to produce this rather easy-to-spot counterfeit.

As always, however, get out the magnifying glass to be sure. An examination of Dale Murphy's name and team are all that is necessary to brand this card a fake. On a genuine Murphy rookie, his name should appear in solid black letters, and his team name in solid magenta letters. The counterfeit renders these words as a composite of tiny color dots.

The counterfeit's back lacks the contrast of an original as a result of the green ink being printed over a screened black pattern designed to make the thin white cardboard stock of the fake look like the traditional gray Topps cardstock.

The black "Reprint" which appears on the back of the specimen photographed here may not be present on all cards encountered in buy and sell transactions.

No photo available

Genuine   **Counterfeit**

An overall fuzzy appearance — front and back — makes this counterfeit look suspicious to an experienced eye.

Examination of the design details with a magnifying glass reveals sure evidence of the counterfeit's status.

Easy differentiation between real and fake on this card can be made by examining the Topps logo inside the baseball at lower left. Those letters on a genuine card will be clean, solid black; on the counterfeit, they are composed of many dots, giving a fuzzy appearance. Similar evi-

dence can be seen in the magenta color of the player's name and the seams of the ball, and the purple color bar at bottom.

On back, a black printed screen has been used to simulate the gray cardboard of a Topps original and hide the white cardboard on which the fake was printed.

The black "Reprint" which appears on the back of the card shown here may not be present on all cards encountered in the hobby market.

Genuine

Counterfeit

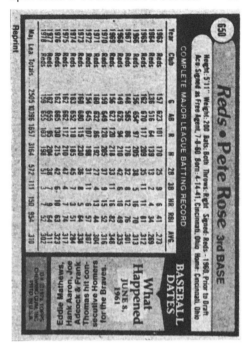

An overall fuzzy appearance — front and back — makes this counterfeit look suspicious to an experienced eye.

Examination of the design details with a magnifying glass reveals sure evidence of the counterfeit's status.

Easy differentiation between real and fake on this card can be made by examining the Topps logo inside the baseball at lower left. Those letters on a genuine card will be clean, solid black; on the counterfeit, they are composed of many dots,

giving a fuzzy appearance. Similar evidence can be seen in the letters of the All Star designation, the player's name and position and the team name.

On back, a black printed screen has been used to simulate the gray cardboard of a Topps original and hide the white cardboard on which the fake was printed.

The black "Reprint" which appears on the back of the card shown here may not be present on all cards encountered in the hobby market.

Genuine

Counterfeit

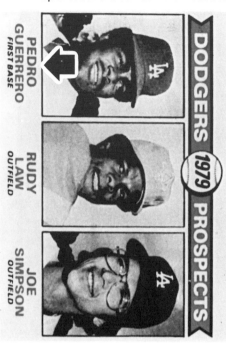

Despite the fact the player photos are black-and-white, this counterfeit is no more deceptive than the others in this "series."

Examination of the color design details with a magnifying glass reveals sure evidence of the counterfeit's status.

Easy differentiation between real and fake on this card can be made by examining the players' names and positions on the front of the card.

Those letters on a genuine card will be clean, solid blue (names) and black (position); on the counterfeit, they are composed of many dots, giving a fuzzy appearance. Similar evidence can be seen in the letters of "DODGERS 1979 PROSPECTS".

On back, a black printed screen has been used to simulate the gray cardboard of a Topps original and hide the white cardboard on which the fake was printed.

The black "Reprint" which appears on the back of the card shown here may not be present on all cards encountered.

Genuine

Counterfeit

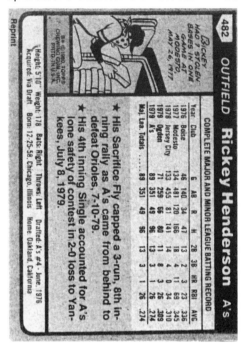

The fuzzy photo and lettering on the front of this counterfeit should put most hobbyists on warning that more detailed examination is needed.

Using a magnifying glass to examine the lettering will provide definite proof that this card is a phony. On a genuine card, such details as the black borders of the frame line, the player's name, position and facsimile autograph, the green position designation and the yellow "A's" should show up as solid colors with edges that end crisply and cleanly at the respec-

tive backgrounds. On this counterfeit, the letters and other color design elements are composed of many tiny color dots, giving them a ragged look at the edges. The back is fairly deceptive, although close examination will show a pattern of gray dots has been printed on the white cardboard to simulate the genuine Topps card stock.

The black "Reprint" which appears on the back of the card shown here may not be present on all cards encountered.

Genuine

Counterfeit

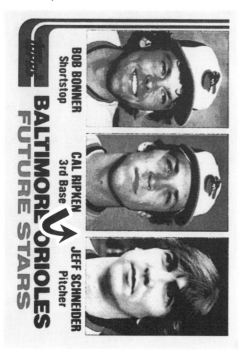
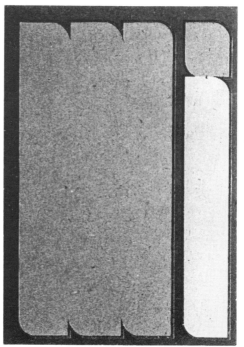

One of the more frequently encountered counterfeits, this phony Ripken rookie is too often thought to be an error card, missing the typography on the back. While there have been reports of a version of this counterfeit being seen with back printing, they have yet to be verified.

For the time being, then, the absence of the printed wording on the card's back is irrefutable proof of its bogus nature.

As a double-check, however, take a magnifying glass to the front of the card.

The color printing is excellent on this counterfeit. An easy means of detection, however, can be found in the black borders which surround the portraits of the Orioles.

On a genuine card, those black boxes will be made up of clean, solid lines. On the counterfeit, the lines are rendered as fuzzy black structures made up of numerous tiny dots.

This counterfeit is often seen as an eight-card sheet, usually offered as some sort of test issue.

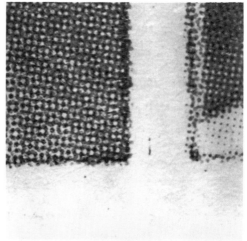

Genuine   **Counterfeit**

	Team Name	Bat Avg	Games	At Bat	Hits	Runs	2B	3B	HR	RBI	Steal	Walk	SO
1983	Cubs	176	23	51	9	6	1	0	1	1		0	21
Career		176	23	51	9	6	1	0	1	1		0	21

JOSEPH CARTER ④① Born: March 7, 1960. Home: Oklahoma City, Okla. Ht: 6'3" Wgt: 215 Bats: Right Throws: Right ©1983 Donruss Printed in USA *Denotes Led League

RECENT MAJOR LEAGUE PERFORMANCE

CAREER HIGHLIGHTS

Luckily, this particular counterfeit is rarely encountered, since it is good enough to fool most viewers without detailed study. The front of the counterfeit is much better than the back, which exhibits a yellowish cast to the green color bars and which has seen a too-heavy application of black ink, bloating the individual letters of the typography.

Unlike the '84 Donruss Mattingly counterfeit, which has poor replication of the logo, the Carter counterfeit has a very passable logo. Examination with a magnifying lens should be concentrated on the white letters of "RATED ROOKIE", the red stripes above and below that notation and the red stripe at bottom which bears the player's name and position. The white letters will be pure and clean on a genuine card, and the red stripes will be solid red. On the fake, there are many tiny blue dots in these areas. On the fake, the yellow letters of the name and position are fuzzy at the edges, rather than ending cleanly at the red background.

Genuine

Counterfeit

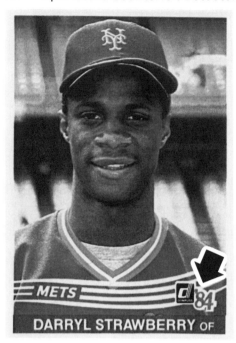

An extremely deceptive counterfeit, this is one of a handful of cards for which 5X magnification is barely adequate for detection of counterfeit "fingerprints."

As with the '84 Mattingly, examination of the logo area at lower right is recommended. On a genuine card printed with decent color registration, the white outline of the "'84" should be devoid of extraneous color dots. The counterfeit — under strong magnification — exhibits a smattering of tiny red and blue dots scattered throughout the white area. Simi-

larly, the player's name on a genuine card will be solid yellow, with only a very occasional intrusive red dot near the edges. On the counterfeit, the name is rife with tiny red and green dots.

On genuine cards that are printed in less than perfect registration, red, yellow or blue dots may occasionally be found in these areas, but they will always be in a pattern consistent with the nearest design elements, rather than scattered at random.

Genuine

Counterfeit

One of the most widespread counterfeits, production was traced to a Florida print shop whose operator was told the cards were being reproduced by a relative of Mattingly's for use as party favors.

At first glance, especially with a genuine card available for comparison, this counterfeit should raise a warning flag. The front borders are more eggshell white than pure white and the surface has an unnaturally smooth gloss. Such subjective observations, however, can never be relied upon to positively identify a counterfeit.

Examination with a magnifying lens offers proof of this card's status through study of the Donruss logo at lower right. On a genuine card, the white outline around the black box and the '''84'', along with the fancy "d" will be clear and clean. On the counterfeit there are many tiny black dots in these areas. Also, the counterfeit's rendition of the small "DONRUSS" in the logo box is fuzzy, with barely distinguishable letters.

Genuine

Counterfeit

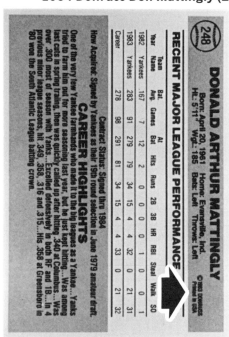

Year	Team Name	Bat. Avg.	Games	At Bat	Hits	Runs	2B	3B	HR	RBI	Steal	Walk	SO
1982	Yankees	.167	7	12	2	0	0	0	0	1	0	0	1
1983	Yankees	.283	91	279	79	34	15	4	4	32	0	21	31
Career		.278	98	291	81	34	15	4	4	33	0	21	32

DONALD ARTHUR MATTINGLY

Born: April 20, 1961   Home: Evansville, Ind.
Ht: 5'11"   Wgt: 185   Bats: Left   Throws: Left

248

RECENT MAJOR LEAGUE PERFORMANCE

CAREER HIGHLIGHTS

One of the very few Yankee farmhands who made it to the big leagues as a Yankee... Yanks tried to farm him out for more seasoning last year, but he just kept hitting...340 at Columbus....Was among last cuts in spring training, then was quickly called up after hitting .340 at Columbus....Was over .300 most of season with Yanks... Excelled defensively in both RF and 1B...In 4 previous minor league seasons, hit .349, .358, .316 and .315...His .358 at Greensboro in '80 won the South Atlantic League batting crown.

How Acquired: Signed by Yankees as their 19th round selection in June 1979 amateur draft.

Contract Status: Signed thru 1984

©1983 DONRUSS   Printed in USA

Much more dangerous than the other known '84 Donruss Mattingly counterfeit, this version also first surfaced in Florida, in November, 1991. It is among the most difficult counterfeits to detect, partially because its weight is within the tolerances of a genuine '84 Donruss card.

The back of a suspected card is the best area of examination, specifically the copyright notice at the upper-right. On a genuine card, all of the letters and numerals stand independently. The counterfeit shows many of these elements run together, touching one or both of the neighboring letters or numerals.

On front, examination with a magnifying

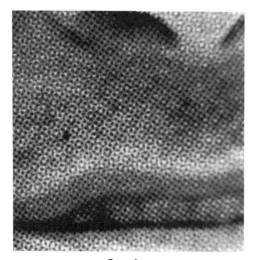

Genuine

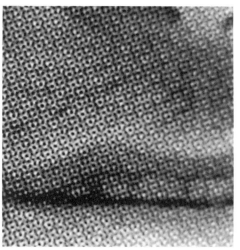

Counterfeit

 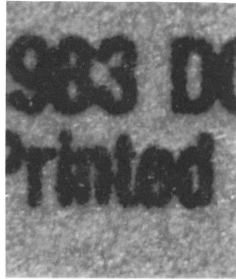

Genuine   **Counterfeit**

glass will reveal flaws in two areas of the counterfeit. The wavy gold lines which contain the team name, as well as the letters of "YANKEES" on a genuine card exhibit fairly clean edges. On the counterfeit, these edges are much rougher.

What appears to be a printing flaw on genuine cards can also be used as a diagnostic. All genuine cards examined show a black spot on Mattingly's upper lip, just above the tooth that is farthest to the viewer's left. In the reproduction process, the counterfeit rendered this dot as a broken pattern of smaller dots, making it virtually invisible to the naked eye.

Each of these areas requires careful study to differentiate between a good and a bad card, and it is especially useful to have a known genuine Mattingly available for comparison.

This dangerous fake can be readily identified by persons with access to a microscope by the presence of black printing dots where they do not exist on a genuine card. These areas include the highlighted areas of the player's neck and right ear lobe, and the wavy gold stripes to the left of the "Y" in "YANKEES".

Genuine   **Counterfeit**

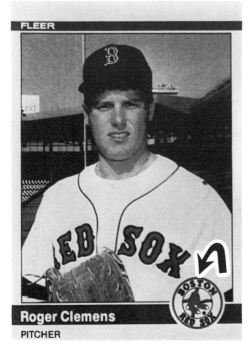

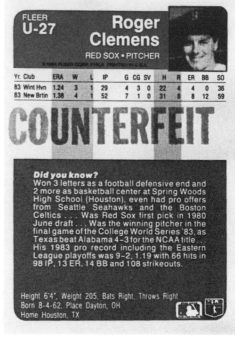

As with the known Gooden and Puckett counterfeits from this scarce and valuable edition, the Clemens counterfeit is most easily detected by close examination of the Red Sox logo on the front of the card.

Seen through a good magnifying glass, the counterfeit will exhibit a pattern of tiny blue dots both in the carmine hose themselves, and in what is supposed to be the pure white background of the baseball and the surrounding type circle. On a gen-

uine 1984 Fleer Update card, the socks and the white area will be without these extraneous dots.

It is interesting to note that the Major League Players Association logo at the lower-right on the counterfeit's back has been "improved," with a new, bolder white outline to the shield.

A "COUNTERFEIT" stamp has been added to the back of the specimen photographed here.

Genuine

Counterfeit

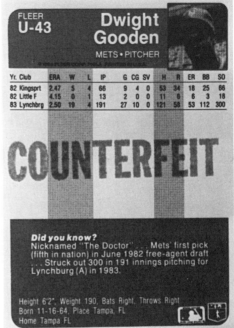

At first glance a very deceptive counterfeit, a person with a keen eye for color might detect a more purple cast to the horizontal stripes on the front of this card, but ink color should never be used as a sole indicator of genuineness or lack thereof. Thankfully, with a good magnifying glass, even those whose chromatic acuity approaches color blindness can detect this counterfeit.

The key is the Mets logo at lower-right on the front. On a genuine card, the white background behind the skyline will contain no dot structure. On the counterfeit, the New York sky is filled with tiny dark dots. These dots can also be seen in the "METS" lettering on the phony, but not on the genuine card.

It is interesting to note that the Players Association logo on the counterfeit's back has been "improved," with a bolder white outline to the shield.

The specimen photographed here bears a "COUNTERFEIT" stamp that will not be seen in the marketplace.

Genuine

Counterfeit

Kirby Puckett
OUTFIELD

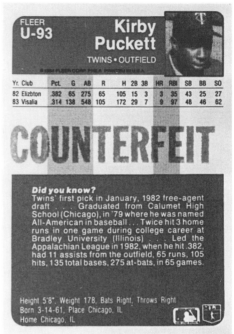

FLEER U-93	Kirby Puckett											
	TWINS • OUTFIELD											

Yr. Club	Pct.	G	AB	R	H	2B	3B	HR	RBI	SB	BB	SO
82 Elizbton	.382	65	275	65	105	15	3	3	35	43	25	27
83 Visalia	.314	138	548	105	172	29	7	9	97	48	46	62

COUNTERFEIT

Did you know?
Twins' first pick in January, 1982 free-agent draft . . . Graduated from Calumet High School (Chicago), in '79 where he was named All-American in baseball . . . Twice hit 3 home runs in one game during college career at Bradley University (Illinois) . . . Led the Appalachian League in 1982, when he hit .382, had 11 assists from the outfield, 65 runs, 105 hits, 135 total bases, 275 at-bats, in 65 games.

Height 5'8", Weight 178, Bats Right, Throws Right
Born 3-14-61, Place Chicago, IL
Home Chicago, IL

As with the known Gooden and Clemens counterfeits from this scarce and valuable edition, the Puckett counterfeit is most easily detected by close examination of the Twins logo on the front of the card.

Seen through a good magnifying glass, the counterfeit will exhibit a pattern of tiny blue dots in the white baseball and uniforms of the cartoon figures, and the red design details and letters of "WIN! TWINS!". On a genuine 1984 Fleer Update card, the white areas of the logo and the red letterings will be devoid of the tell-tale blue dots.

It is interesting to note that the Major League Players Association logo at the lower-right on the counterfeit's back has been "improved," with a new, bolder white outline to the shield.

A "COUNTERFEIT" stamp has been added to the back of the specimen photographed here.

Genuine

Counterfeit

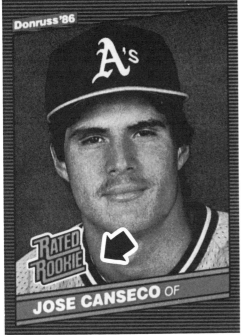

According to hobby lore, genuine Canseco rookies have a "white dot" ¼" above the player's right eye. Actually a pair of parallel scratches, that "dot" vanished when this very deceptive counterfeit was made. Unfortunately, that dot also disappeared when Donruss printed its factory sets.

A similar indicator is the blue stripe under the lower-left corner of the red "Donruss '86" logo. On a genuine wax- or rak-pack card, that stripe extends almost to the "r". On the counterfeit — and on genuine factory-set cards — the blue stripe ends under the "D".

The best test is to study with a magnifying glass the black "TM" to the bottom-right of the "Rated Rookie" logo. Barely visible on a genuine card because it is printed over a very dark green jersey stripe, the letters are solid black lines. On the counterfeit, these letters are rendered fuzzy with a dot structure and little except the right leg of the "M" is visible on the player's neck.

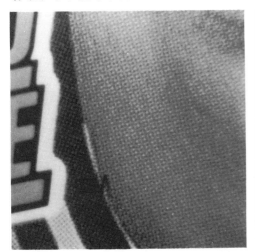

Genuine

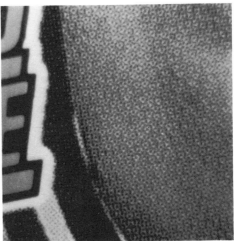

Counterfeit

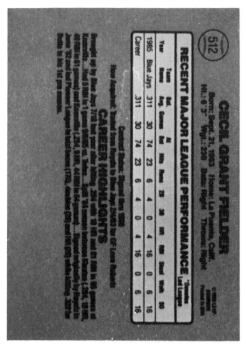

Side-by-side with a genuine card, this counterfeit should fool nobody. The white areas of the color photo on a good card have taken on a yellowish cast on the fake that should alert most viewers.

As always, however, color tint alone should not be relied upon to detect a counterfeit.

The Blue Jays team logo at the lower-left of the card can provide definitive proof under magnification. On a genuine card, the white areas of the circle and the ball will be pure white, and the maple leaf will be almost solid red. On the counterfeit, the white areas of the logo are invaded by a horde of tiny blue, yellow and magenta dots, and the maple leaf is covered with a pattern of dark dots.

Genuine   **Counterfeit**

An excellent counterfeit. The hobby is fortunate the producer of the Ruben Sierra Fleer rookie card did not attempt to create bogus specimens of the more valuable cards in this popular set — at least so far as is known to date. In all likelihood, this card would fool most collectors and dealers because the color finish and focus are not markedly dissimilar from genuine 1987 Fleer baseball cards.

The place to look to be sure you're getting a genuine Sierra rookie — or at least not this particular counterfeit — is the Rangers team logo at lower-right on the front. On the genuine card, the white ball and the red stitching, along with the "Rangers" lettering, will be free of dots. The counterfeit has myriad dots in these areas, rendering the stitching as a pair of fuzzy curved lines, and generally muddying up the other elements of the logo.

Among recent counterfeits, the Fleer Sierra card is very seldom seen — unless a lot of people have unknowingly accepted them as genuine.

Genuine

Counterfeit

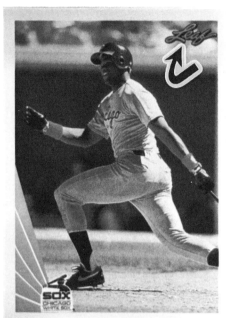

FRANK THOMAS 1B

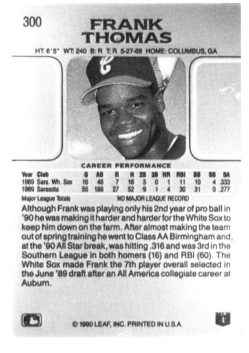

Printed on very thin cardboard, if presented outside of a plastic holder this counterfeit would deceive no one who has ever handled a genuine 1990 Leaf card.

This first known attempt to replicate one of the premium-quality five-color cards might stand a cursory visual once-over, but a close-up examination with a magnifying glass will reveal the counterfeit very easily.

Specifically, a study of the "Leaf" script White Sox in the upper-right corner will show a pattern logo at the lower-left will show of color dots within the letters on the counterfeit, instead of that the pure silver displayed on the genuine card. Similarly, instead of the "CHICAGO WHITE SOX" letters at lower-left being formed of clean red lines, as on the original, those words on the counterfeit are composed of many red dots.

As might be expected, this counterfeit weighs perceptibly less than a genuine Leaf card.

Genuine

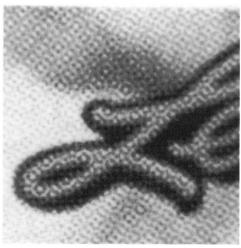

Counterfeit

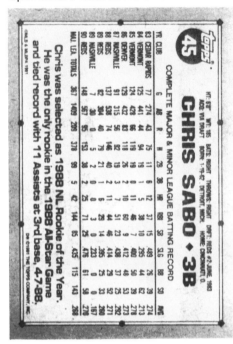

Here we are not dealing with a counterfeit card, but a bogus overprint. Color should never be used alone as a counterfeit detector, but on D.S. cards it's a good place to start. This fake overprint is a more yellow, brassy tone than the Topps-applied design.

Besides being larger than the genuine overprint, the phony lacks the fine details of the true version — the bands around the tree trunk and the coconuts cannot be seen. On the flag, the fake will show no stars, and the stripes are indistinct.

Probably the easiest point of difference to spot this fake overprint is at the bottom tip of the shield. On a genuine Desert Shield overprint, the tip of the shield is blunt, almost rounded. The tip of the shield on this type of counterfeit appears as a pair of sharp points.

It should be assumed that all cards in the 1991 Topps set can be found with the fake overprint, but naturally high-value rookie and star cards will be most often encountered.

Genuine

Counterfeit

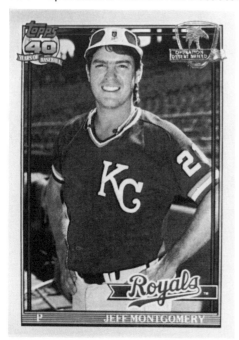

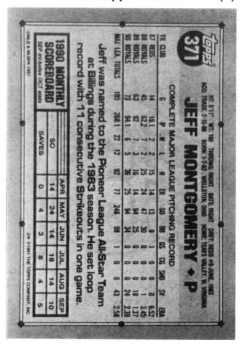

A more dangerous fake than the first variety, this type of counterfeit gold foil Desert Shield overprint features a round-bottom shield, much like the genuine. As with the first counterfeit, the more brassy, yellowish gold color of the foil differs from the genuine Topps imprint.

A fine measurement is one way to determine this counterfeit. A genuine D.S. imprint measures 15mm from the left edge of the banner to the tip of the flag. This type of counterfeit has a measurement of 16mm in that area.

Visually, this type of fake overprint can be discerned by checking the details of the palm tree in the logo. On a genuine card, the background printing of the card itself will show through in the areas that represent the coconuts and the tree trunk. The gold leaf of the phony overprint fully covers the background printing.

It should be assumed that all cards in the 1991 Topps set can be found with the fake overprint, but naturally high-value rookie and star cards will be most often encountered.

Genuine

Counterfeit

Genuine

Counterfeit

There is no challenge to identifying this version of the counterfeit 1988 Cal Cards Ken Griffey Jr. minor league card.

On the genuine card, issued as part of a San Bernardino Spirit team set, the color photo of Griffey shows him in the team's dark blue jersey, hunched over with his hands on his thighs.

The counterfeit depicts Griffey in a home white uniform, in a throwing pose.

Definitely more challenging to identify than the other known forgery of the 1988 Cal Cards Griffey minor league card.

On the genuine card, issued as part of a San Bernardino Spirit team set, all of the white lettering down the sides and at the bottom of the card's front will be pure white when examined under magnifica-tion.

This counterfeit exhibits a dot pattern within these letters when viewed close-up.

Since the rest of the team set was not counterfeited, it pays to be especially wary when offered this card as a single, rather than part of a complete set.

Genuine

Counterfeit

Genuine   **Counterfeit**

There is no challenge to identifying the counterfeit 1986 Memphis Chicks Bo Jackson minor league cards.

On the genuine card, issued as part of a team set, the color photo of Jackson shows him in the team's home white uniform, with "Chicks" visible across the chest.

The counterfeit depicts Jackson in a road uniform, with "Memphis" across the chest and can be found in both silver-border and gold-border versions, simulating the genuine issues.

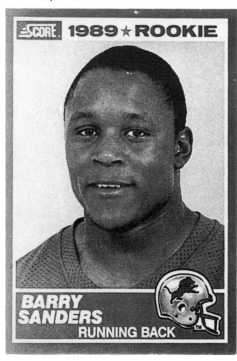

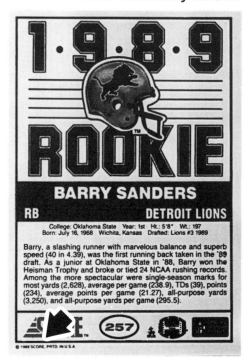

Viewed with the unaided eye, this counterfeit could be quite deceptive. However, having been warned of the existence of a fake, quick examination with a magnifying lens will protect any prospective purchaser.

In the process of re-screening a genuine Sanders rookie card to create printing materials for the counterfeit, many of the tiny design details that are seen on the real thing to be composed of clean, solid lines will show up on the counterfeit as a composition of tiny color dots. While many of these could be pointed out, among the quickest and easiest to spot is the tiny green copyright line at the bottom-left of the card's back. The genuine card shows these letters as clean lines, while the counterfeit displays their tell-tale dot structure.

Genuine

Counterfeit

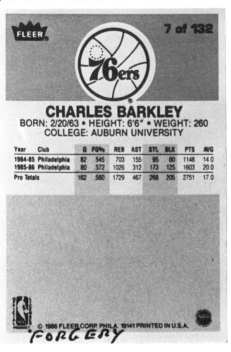

This is one of the toughest counterfeits for which to provide definitive points of difference between real and fake.

One difference centers on a flaw on the genuine card. At the player's left elbow there was an attempt made to clean up a print line extending roughly horizontally from the left bicep to within 1/16th'' of the right border. In re-screening a genuine card to create the counterfeit, the disguised print line disappeared. It's possible, however, that a later generation of the genuine Barkley card could have been printed with the touched-up print line totally removed.

Corroborating evidence can be sought at about the same point in the yellow right border. The counterfeit has a nick in the black frame line at left, exposing a pimple of yellow ink on the counterfeit that is not present on genuine cards.

On back, some of the loops of letters and numbers will be filled in or nearly so on the counterfeit. The ''FORGERY'' penned on the back of the photographed card is unique to this specimen.

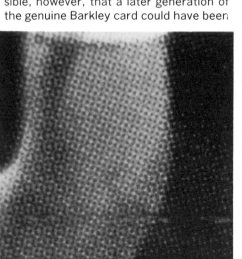

Genuine

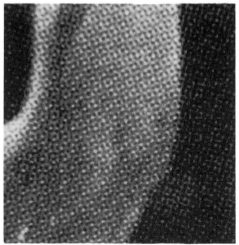

Counterfeit

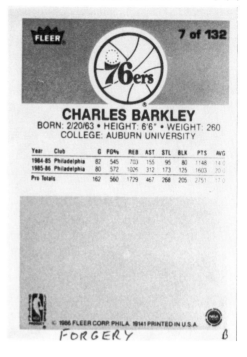

This is by far the easier of the known types of 1986-87 Fleer Barkley counterfeits to spot. This card exhibits its fatal flaw within the crown-and-banner "FLEER PREMIER" logo at the upper-right.

On a genuine card, the word "PRE-MIER" will show its letters as clean, solid black lines. On this counterfeit, the letters (as well as the black borders of the banner) are composed of many tiny black dots.

Like many (but not all) of the 1986-87 Fleer basketball counterfeits, the fine details of the NBA Players Association logo on the back of the card did not reproduce well; the seams of the basketball are missing, and there is a lack of distinctness to the letters around the ball.

The "FORGERY B" penned on the back of the photographed card is unique to this specimen.

Genuine   **Counterfeit**

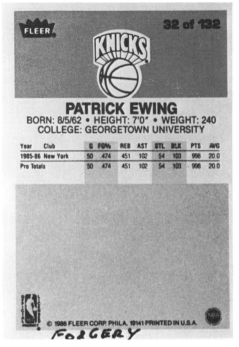

The better of two known Fleer counterfeit Ewing cards. The key to quick, easy detection is worn by the Knicks star, on each wrist. On a genuine card, examination under magnification will reveal hundreds of tiny blue dots giving a subtle hint of color to the wristbands worn by Ewing. This particular counterfeit has no such dots on the wristband. As is frequently the case, this difference cannot be detected by the naked eye, a good magnifying lens is necessary.

A tiny white dot to the left of the "P" in

"PATRICK" on the counterfeit card's front can also be used as a counterfeit indicator.

Unlike most of the 1986-87 Fleer basketball counterfeits, the Fleer logo on front, and the NBA and Players Associations logos on the back of this version are virtually indistinguishable from those on a genuine card.

The counterfeit card shown here has had the word "FORGERY" and letter "A" penned on the back.

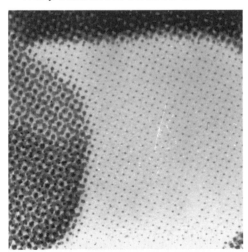

Genuine

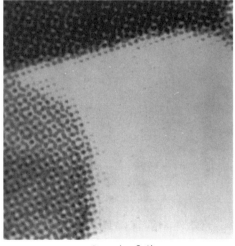

Counterfeit

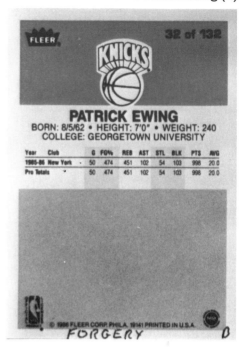

The second type of Ewing counterfeit is best detected by magnification-assisted examination of the crown-and-banner "FLEER / PREMIER " logo in the upper-right corner of the card's front. Instead of the solid black "PREMIER" and lines bordering the yellow banner of the logo, this counterfeit evidences those elements in a myriad of tiny black dots, creating an overall fuzzy appearance.

Unlike the other Ewing fake, this card does have the blue dots in the wristbands.

The back of this counterfeit has a very bad rendition of the NBA Players Association logo at lower-right; virtually none of the letters around the ball are decipherable, and several of the letters of "PLAYERS" inside the ball-logo are filled in with excessive blue ink. The registration mark (®) beneath the NBA logo at lower-left is similarly unidentifiable.

The specimen shown here has had the word "FORGERY" and the letter "B" penned on.

Genuine

Counterfeit

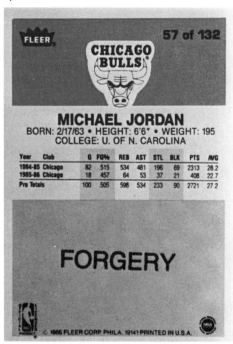

The first of three known counterfeits of the Jordan rookie card is easily and unequivocally detected by examination of the "FLEER / PREMIER " logo in the upper-right corner of the card's front. On a genuine card, the red crown, yellow pattern and black "PREMIER" are made up of solid colors. On this particular Jordan counterfeit, those elements are seen under magnification to contain dot structures, the result of a genuine card having been rescreened to create the necessary printing elements for the counterfeit.

The blue color of the fake card's back is lighter than on a genuine Jordan rookie, especially in the area of the Fleer crown at upper-left. On a genuine card, the crown is actually purple, the result of combining blue and red ink. This Jordan counterfeit shows only the blue ink used in the crown.

The counterfeit card shown here has had the word "FORGERY" stamped on it; do not expect to see such a warning on cards you may be offered for sale.

Genuine

Counterfeit

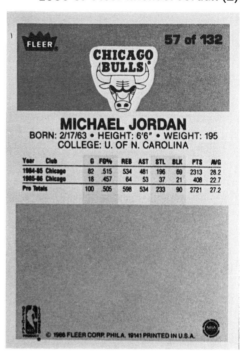

The second identified Jordan rookie counterfeit is somewhat more deceptive than the first, but the area of scrutiny is the same, the "FLEER / PREMIER " logo in the upper-right corner of the card's front. On a genuine card, the black lines which border the yellow panel, and the word "PREMIER" itself are made up of solid colors. On this particular Jordan counterfeit, those elements are seen under magnification to be made up of many tiny black dots, giving the word a fuzzy appearance under magnification.

Unlike the Jordan counterfeit identified as (1), the red crown and yellow panel of the logo do not contain any dot structure on this version.

Like most of the 1986-87 Fleer basketball counterfeits, the NBA Players Association logo at the lower-right on the back is very muddy on this counterfeit. The "seams" of the basketball, usually visible on a genuine card, are all but absent on this phony, as are most of the details of the lettering in and around this logo.

Genuine

Counterfeit

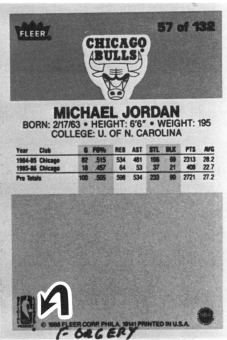

The most deceptive of the three known counterfeit Jordan rookie types. The crown-and-banner "FLEER / PREMIER" logo on the card's front, which is so useful in detecting the other two known Jordan counterfeits, cannot be so readily used as an indicator on this card.

The most reliable signposts of this card's counterfeit status are found on the back, where a too-liberal use of the blue ink tended to clog the fine details of the logos and typography. This is most noticeable in the ® registration mark beneath the NBA logo at lower-left. On a genuine card, the "R" is readily seen; on the counterfeit, it is an indecipherable blob. By contrast, the Players Association logo at lower-right is much better defined on this counterfeit than on most of the fake 1986-87 Fleer basketball cards.

Again, the word "FORGERY" penned in the bottom border of the photographed card is unique to this specimen.

Genuine

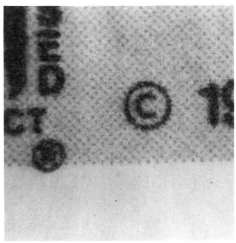

Counterfeit

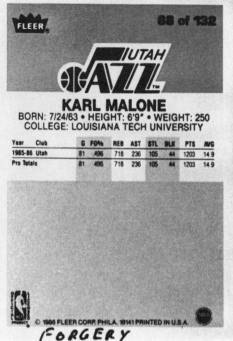

Unlike the majority of 1986-87 Fleer basketball counterfeits, the Fleer crown-and-banner logo cannot be used to detect this counterfeit.

On the front, the best place to check the card is the point of the player's left cheek. On the counterfeit examined, a white spot is visible to the naked eye. However, the reader should be cautioned that insufficient specimens of this type counterfeit have been examined to determine whether this white dot can be used alone as a diagnostic.

On back, the registration (®) and copyright marks (©) near the NBA logo can be used as a double-check. On a genuine card, the "R" and the "C" and the circles around them will be distinct and complete. On the counterfeit, the "R" looks more like a misshapen "K" and the "C" and its circle are incomplete in spots.

The "FORGERY" penned on the back of the photographed card is unique to this specimen.

Genuine

Counterfeit

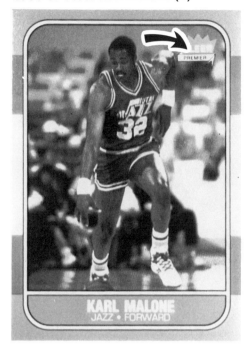

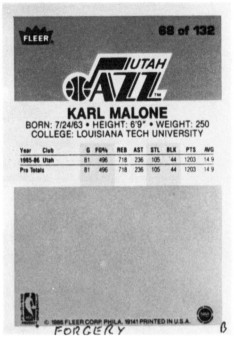

This is by far the easier of the known types of 1986-87 Fleer Malone counterfeits to spot. This card exhibits its fatal flaw within the crown-and-banner "FLEER PREMIER" logo at the upper-right.

On a genuine card, the word "PRE-MIER" will show its letters as clean, solid black lines. On this counterfeit, the letters (as well as the black borders of the banner) are composed of many tiny black dots.

Like many (but not all) of the 1986-87 Fleer basketball counterfeits, the fine details of the NBA Players Association logo on the back of the card did not reproduce well; the seams of the basketball are missing, and there is a lack of distinctness to the letters around the ball.

The "FORGERY B" penned on the back of the photographed card is unique to this specimen.

Genuine

Counterfeit

Genuine

Counterfeit

Counterfeit

On the right side of the card back, the logo of the National Basketball Players Association can be found. On genuine cards, the letters within and around the basketball symbol can be easily distinguished with the use of a magnifying glass. Likewise, the "seams" of the basketball will be readily visible.

Most of the counterfeits can do little but reproduce this logo as a purple blob. The letters around the ball are indecipherable, and usually there are several missing or misshapen letters among "PLAYERS" inside the ball. In most cases there will be little or no trace of the ball's seams.

Because this appears to be a set that will be subject to future counterfeits as the value of the scarce genuine cards rises, hobbyists will be well advised to study these card-back design details whenever considering purchase of a high-value card from the 1986-87 Fleer set.

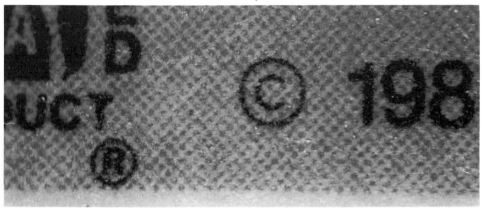

Genuine

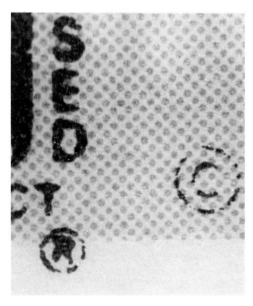

Counterfeit   **Counterfeit**

Counterfeit 1986-87 Fleer backs

Because most of the known 1986-87 Fleer basketball counterfeits exhibit diagnostics that are more easily seen, described and/or photographed, little was said about the card backs.

In most cases, the counterfeits of this Fleer issue bear markedly flawed design details on the card backs. This is the result of the counterfeiters having to reproduce design details that are already very small.

On genuine Fleer cards, the registration (®) and copyright (©) marks at the bottom-left of the backs will virtually always be perfectly clear and legible upon close examination with a magnifying glass. Both the letters and the circles will be complete.

On most of the counterfeits, these marks are rendered as either incomplete (most often the ©) or over-inked, blurred images (®).

Visually a very deceptive counterfeit.

The best place to determine good from bad is to examine under magnification the card number "353" in the upper-left corner of the card's back.

On a genuine card these numerals are clean and white. On the counterfeit, the numerals' edges appear fuzzy. On close examination, stray print dots of blue, red and yellow can be found scattered throughout the numbers on the fake.

It is also interesting to note that the fine type at the bottom of the card back is actually cleaner on the counterfeit. On a genuine card, many of the letters in those lines are run together. Surprisingly, on this counterfeit, most of the letters stand distinctly apart. This cleaner typography on the counterfeit is apparently the result of the counterfeiters having these lines re-set. In doing so, however, the copyright line at the bottom was rendered somewhat longer than the line on the genuine card. This line measures 44.5mm on a real card, while on the counterfeit, the line measures 46mm.

Genuine

Counterfeit

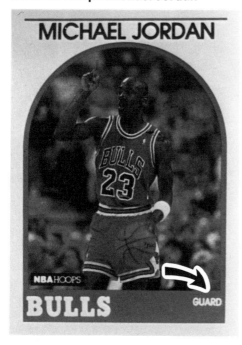

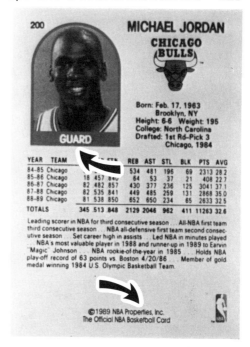

This is a very deceptive counterfeit, perhaps the work of the same parties responsible for the Type 2 Hoops David Robinson counterfeit.

On this card, the best areas for examination are the white words "GUARD" at the lower-right of the front, and under the portrait on the back. In each case, the counterfeit shows letters that are joined rather than separated as on a genuine card.

Under magnification, the "GUARD" on front of a counterfeit will show the "G" and "U" connected near the crossbar of the "G". On back, the counterfeit has the "R" and "D" connected near the top. On a genuine card, only the "A" and "R" are connected, near the bottom, on both front and back.

Another indicator of status can be found in the copyright notice on the back. On a genuine card, many of the letters and numbers in both lines are run together. Surprisingly, on this counterfeit, the letters and numbers do not connect, except at the "rt" of "Properties", and the "ff" of "Official". This cleaner typography on the counterfeit is apparently the result of the counterfeiters having these lines re-set with a new, slightly lighter,

Genuine

Counterfeit

Genuine

Counterfeit

typeface. In doing so, however, the resulting copyright lines are somewhat longer than the lines on the genuine card. The bottom line of a genuine card, "The Official NBA Basketball Card", will measure 23mm. On the counterfeit, the line measures 24mm.

Genuine

Counterfeit

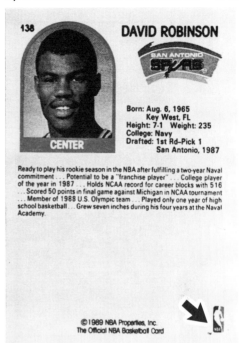

The "lesser of two evils," the first type of two known fake Hoops Robinson rookies should be easily spotted on the basis of its overall appearance. The colors — front and back — are darker and coarser than on a genuine card. However, as color can never be reliably used by itself to establish the status of a questioned card, a closer look is necessary.

In this case, the closer look is best concentrated on the back of the card; specifically on the NBA logo at lower-right. On a genuine card the white "NBA" initials and the black "TM" will stand out clearly as distinct individual letters. On this type of counterfeit, these letters (especially the white "NBA") are blurred and virtually indistinguishable.

Genuine

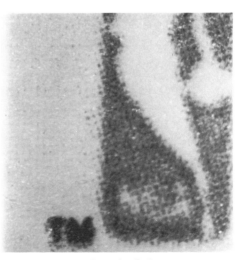

Counterfeit

DAVID ROBINSON

138

Born: Aug. 6, 1965
Key West, FL
Height: 7-1   Weight: 235
College: Navy
Drafted: 1st Rd–Pick 1
San Antonio, 1987

CENTER

Ready to play his rookie season in the NBA after fulfilling a two-year Naval commitment . . . Potential to be a "franchise player" . . . College player of the year in 1987 . . . Holds NCAA record for career blocks with 516 . . . Scored 50 points in final game against Michigan in NCAA tournament . . . Member of 1988 U.S. Olympic team . . . Played only one year of high school basketball . . . Grew seven inches during his four years at the Naval Academy.

©1989 NBA Properties, Inc.
The Official NBA Basketball Card

By far the scarier of two known types of counterfeit Hoops Robinson rookies, it will take a good magnifying lens to identify this particular fake.

There is an irregularity in one of the letters of the player's name at top that is worth mention. Specficially, the counterfeit shows a tiny white notch near the top of the slanting leg of the "R".

A second indicator — again requiring high magnification to detect — is seen in the "B" of the "NBA Hoops" logo in the lower-right corner of the photo. On a gen-

uine card, that letter (and all the others) will be pure white against the black background. On the counterfeit, the holes formed by the loops of the "B" will show red ink — it looks like nothing so much as blood oozing out of the two "bullet holes" in the "B". Depending on the printing registration of the specific example of the counterfeit being viewed, a few other extraneous red dots may be visible at the edges of some of the other letters in this logo.

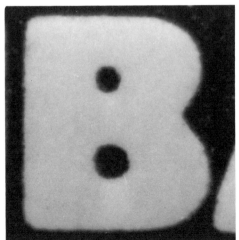

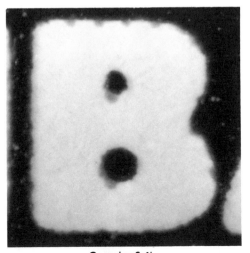

| Genuine | Counterfeit |

Genuine   Counterfeit

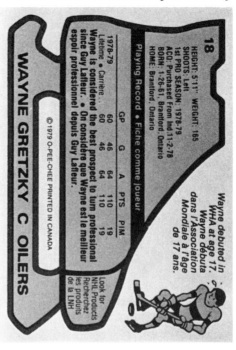

Viewed with the naked eye, the Gretzky rookie counterfeit can be considered fairly deceptive. That illusion vanishes with the application of a magnifying lens to the front of the card. Many of the design elements on the front of the counterfeit can be seen under magnification to be composed of tiny dots, rather than the solid lines and colors of the genuine card.

This is easily noted in such areas as the black frame lines around the photo and designs, the black "EDMONTON", the orange "OILERS" and flame of the team logo, and the white letters of the player's name and position.

The ice in the photo can also be used to determine the status of a questioned card. On the genuine card, the ice is clean and white. On the counterfeit, there are thousands of tiny blue dots visible on the ice.

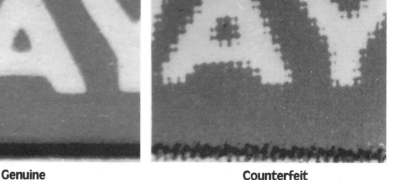

Genuine   **Counterfeit**

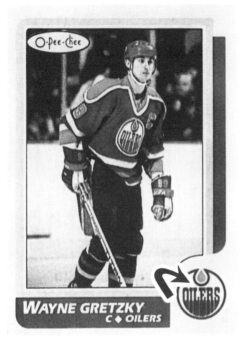

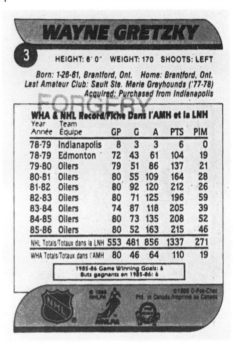

Only with a quick glance by the unaided eye would an experienced hockey card enthusiast be taken in by this counterfeit.

Because an original card was re-screened to create printing materials for the counterfeit, the resulting bogus card shows printers' dots in all sorts of places where they will never appear on the genuine version.

The re-screening has resulted in tiny blue dots in what are supposed to be the card's pure white borders and in the player's name, position letter and team in the in the bottom blue stripe. There are also big black dots making up the O-Pee-Chee brand name in the logo at upper-left. Those letters should be clear, clean black lines.

Similarly, the blue and orange Oilers logo at lower-right is composed of color dots rather than solid structures.

The stamped ''FORGERY'' on the back of the card photographed is unique to that specimen.

Genuine

Counterfeit

53

FORGERY

WAYNE GRETZKY ♦ Center / Centre

Height: 6'0"
Weight: 170
Shoots: L
Born: 1-26-61, Brantford, Ont.   Home: Brantford, Ont.
Last Amateur Club: Sault Ste. Marie Greyhounds (1977-78)
Acquired: Purchased from Indianapolis

WHA & NHL Record/Fiche dans l'AMH et la LNH

Year	Team	GP	G	A	PTS	PIM
78-79	INDIANAPOLIS	8	6	3	9	0
78-79	EDMONTON	72	43	61	104	19
79-80	OILERS	79	51	86	137	21
80-81	OILERS	80	55	109	164	28
81-82	OILERS	80	92	120	212	26
82-83	OILERS	79	71	125	196	59
83-84	OILERS	74	87	118	205	39
84-85	OILERS	80	73	135	208	52
85-86	OILERS	80	52	163	215	46
86-87	OILERS	79	62	121	183	28
WHA Totals/Totaux dans l'AMH		80	46	64	110	19
NHL Totals/Totaux dans la LNH		632	543	977	1520	298

1986-87 Game Winning Goals: 4 / Buts gagnants marqués en 1986-87: 4
Wayne led NHL in goals, assists, points, and short-handed goals (7). • Wayne a été le meneur de la LNH pour les buts, assistances, points et buts marqués en désavantage numérique (7).

© 1987 O-Pee-Chee Ptd. in Canada/Imprimé au Canada

Not a particularly deceptive counterfeit, except perhaps when viewed with the unaided eye in a plastic holder. A tip-off to the card's counterfeit status should come from the unnatural glossy finish on the front of the card.

More objectively, a close examination of the card front with a magnifying glass will reveal the counterfeit on the basis of printing dots where they will never appear on a genuine card — in the white border. This is the only counterfeit examined to date which exhibits a dot pattern in what is supposed to be a white border. The yellow triangle at lower-left which has the player's position indicated also exhibits background dots on the counterfeit that are not present on the genuine card.

Perhaps the easiest extraneous dots to spot are in the black oval OPC logo at upper-left. On the genuine card the white letters of the brand name should be pure white. On the counterfeit, these letters have been invaded by red and blue color dots.

Genuine

Counterfeit

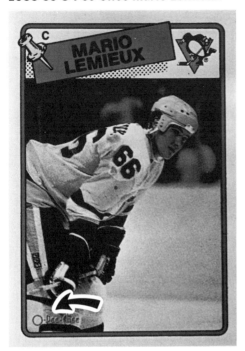

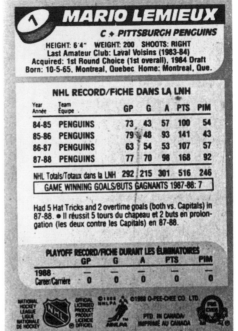

One of a quintet of very skillful counterfeit 1988-89 OPC hockey cards.

Unlike some of the counterfeits of earlier OPC cards, which show printers' dots in all sorts of places where they will never appear on the genuine card, this group requires close examination of specific areas with a good magnifying glass to spot the counterfeiter's mistakes.

On this card, the best area for examination is the blue O-Pee-Chee logo in the lower-left corner. Off-register placement of the blue letters (they are low and to the right) has left a visible group of "shadow" letters composed of blue dots above and to the right. These shadow structures are the remainder of the original logo that was re-screened from a genuine card to create printing materials for the counterfeit.

While it cannot be used as a diagnostic, it is worth noting that genuine specimens of 1988-89 OPC are quite often found with one or more edges fairly roughly cut, while all counterfeits seen have well-cut edges all around.

Genuine

Counterfeit

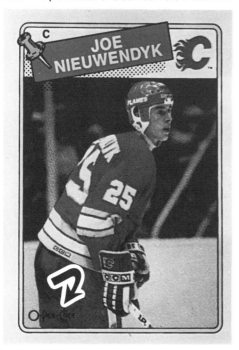

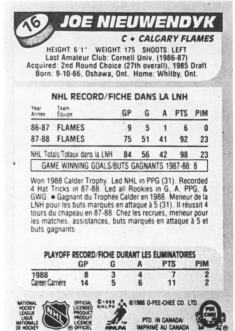

This is one of five very dangerous counterfeit 1988-89 OPC hockey cards. This group requires close examination of specific areas with a good magnifying glass to spot the counterfeiter's mistakes.

On this card, the best area for examination is the black O-Pee-Chee logo in the lower-left corner. Rather than being printed as clean, solid black letters, the "O-Pee-Chee" on the counterfeit is composed of letters made up of many small black dots.

The same is true for the black dots in the upper-left of the picture, which are supposed to represent the "shadow" of the red name box. On an original card these dots would be rendered as single black dots. On this counterfeit, they are made up of many smaller dots.

While it cannot be used as a diagnostic, it is worth noting that genuine specimens of 1988-89 OPC are quite often found with one or more edges fairly roughly cut, while all counterfeits seen have well-cut edges all around.

Genuine

Counterfeit

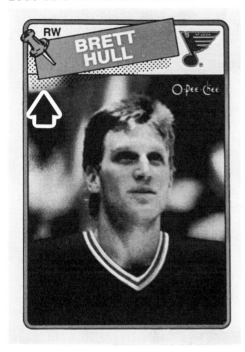

This is one of five very dangerous counterfeit 1988-89 OPC hockey cards.

Unlike some of the counterfeits of earlier OPC cards, which show printers' dots in all sorts of places where they will never appear on the genuine card, this group requires close examination of specific areas with a good magnifying glass to spot the counterfeiter's mistakes.

On this card, the best area for examination is the pattern of black dots in the upper-left of the picture, which is supposed to represent the "shadow" of the blue name box. On an original card these dots would be rendered as single solid black elements. On this counterfeit, each dot is made up of many smaller dots.

While it cannot be used as a diagnostic, it is worth noting that genuine specimens of 1988-89 OPC are quite often found with one or more edges fairly roughly cut, while all counterfeits seen have well-cut edges all around.

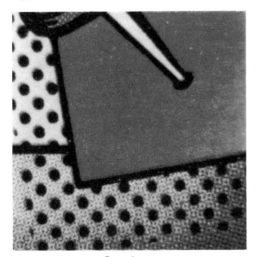

Genuine

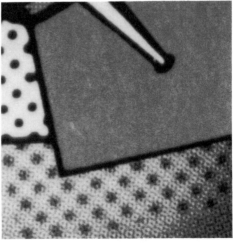

Counterfeit

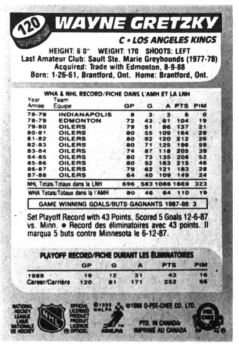

This is hardest to spot among a quintet of dangerous counterfeit 1988-89 OPC hockey cards.

On this card, the best area for examination is the series of square black dots intended to represent a shadow beneath the yellow name box. Specifically, the uppermost squares to the left of the push-pin should be studied under magnification. On the counterfeit, many of the squares are poorly formed, but the real key is the top square in the row third from the left of the name box; it has a bar that

extends to the left, touching the black photo-frame line. On a genuine card, there is no such bar, though the square itself does touch the frame line. Also note on the genuine card that there is a partial black square printed into the purple border, above and to the left of the previously mentioned square.

While it cannot be used as a diagnostic, it is worth noting that genuine 1988-89 OPC are often found with one or more roughly cut edges, while all counterfeits seen have well-cut edges all around.

Genuine

Counterfeit

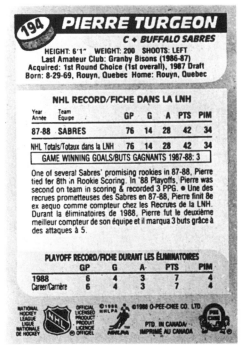

This is one of series of five very dangerous counterfeit 1988-89 OPC hockey cards.

Unlike some of the counterfeits of earlier OPC cards, which show printers' dots in all sorts of places where they will never appear on the genuine card, this group requires close examination of specific areas with a good magnifying glass to spot the counterfeiter's mistakes.

On this card, the best area for examination is the white O-Pee-Chee logo in the upper-right corner of the photo. On a genuine card, the letters of the brand name should be clean and white when viewed under magnification. On this counterfeit, the letters will be seen to be infected with many small printers' color dots.

While it cannot be used as a diagnostic, it is worth noting that genuine specimens of 1988-89 OPC are quite often found with one or more edges fairly roughly cut, while all counterfeits seen have well-cut edges all around.

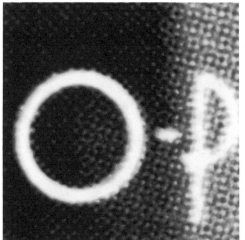

Genuine

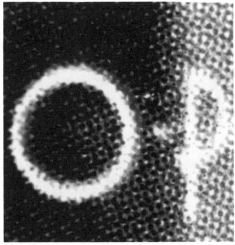

Counterfeit

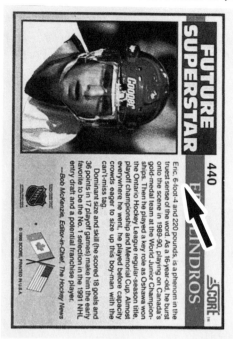

Visually a fairly deceptive counterfeit, this is one example of a fake that is so far out of bounds on card weight as to raise immediate suspicions — it is over 40% heavier than a genuine card. This difference is easily perceived when handling the card outside of any type of plastic holder.

There is also a very easily detected visual indicator of this card's counterfeit status. The black type on the back of card is rendered on this counterfeit in a series of tiny dots, rather than as the clean black lines found on a genuine card. This flaw is not visible to the naked eye, requiring the aid of a magnifying glass. The rescreening of the type on a genuine card has produced indecipherable legends above and below the NHL shield.

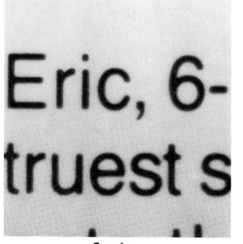

Genuine

Counterfeit

The second known type of Lindros counterfeit is also a very deceptive card.

While this counterfeit, too, varies in weight, the slightly more than 10% difference (the counterfeit is lighter than a genuine 1990-91 Score hockey card) is not significant enough to be discerned except by very precise scales.

Fortunately, there is an easily detected flaw, again on the back of the card. Whereas the red bars and maple leaf of the Canadian flag will be printed on a genuine card in solid red, the counterfeit card displays these elements with a pattern of tiny yellow dots in the red areas.

Genuine

Counterfeit

SERGEI FEDOROV
RED WINGS • CENTER/CENTRE

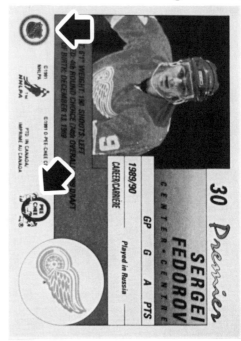

To an experienced hockey card collector, something is "not right" about the look of the three known counterfeited cards in this set. However, since such things as the richness of color and the shade of the gold band at top are subjective, they cannot be reliably used as definite indicators of genuine or counterfeit status.

Rather, flip the card over and with a magnifying glass, examine the O-Pee-Chee logo to the lower-left of the Red Wings logo. On a genuine card, the boy at left will be a "blond", having three shocks of white hair, separated by black lines. On the counterfeit, the boy has all-black hair. Similarly, the boy lazing in the "O" of a genuine card has a complete black line defining the outline of his left leg. On the counterfeit, part of that line is missing.

Another indicator is found in the letters of the NHL logo at lower-left. The white letters in the outer ring are readable on a genuine card, but indecipherable on the fake. Again, use a good magnifier.

Genuine

Counterfeit

Genuine   **Counterfeit**

Genuine   **Counterfeit**

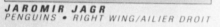

JAROMIR JAGR
PENGUINS • RIGHT WING/AILIER DROIT

To an experienced hockey card collector, something is "not right" about the look of the three known counterfeited cards in this set. However, since such things as the richness of color and the shade of the gold band at top are subjective, they cannot be reliably used as definite indicators of genuine or counterfeit status.

Rather, flip the card over and with a magnifying glass, examine the O-Pee-Chee logo to the lower-left of the Penguins logo. On a genuine card, the boy at left will be a "blond", having three shocks of white hair, separated by black lines. On the counterfeit, the boy has all-black hair. Similarly, the boy lazing in the "O" of a genuine card has a complete black line defining the outline of his left leg. On the counterfeit, part of that line is missing.

Another indicator is found in the letters of the NHL logo at lower-left. The white letters in the outer ring are readable on a genuine card, but indecipherable on the fake. Again, use a good magnifier.

Genuine   **Counterfeit**

Genuine   **Counterfeit**

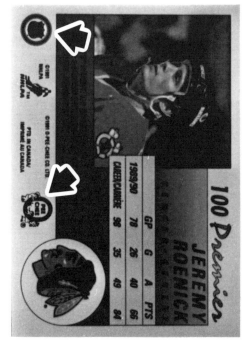

To an experienced hockey card collector, something is "not right" about the look of the three known counterfeited cards in this set. However, since such things as the richness of color and the shade of the gold band at top are subjective, they cannot be reliably used as definite indicators of genuine or counterfeit status.

Rather, flip the card over and with a magnifying glass, examine the O-Pee-Chee logo to the lower-left of the Blackhawks logo. On a genuine card, the boy at left will be a "blond", having three shocks of white hair, separated by black lines. On the counterfeit, the boy has all-black hair. Similarly, the boy lazing in the "O" of a genuine card has a complete black line defining the outline of his left leg. On the counterfeit, part of that line is missing.

Another indicator is found in the letters of the NHL logo at lower-left. The white letters in the outer ring are readable on a genuine card, but indecipherable on the fake. Again, use a good magnifier.

Genuine

Counterfeit

Genuine

Counterfeit

Genuine

Counterfeit

Late additions

A recent spate of counterfeit cards which has hit Chicago indicates the economics of counterfeiting may be changing.

Most of the counterfeits presented in the main body of this book reproduce cards with current retail values in excess of $50. Many of the genuine cards which have been faked sell for hundreds — even thousands — of dollars.

Four of the five most recently discovered counterfeits detailed in these last-minute additional pages are of cards which have catalog values of $35 or less. Three of them — the '87 Donruss Canseco and the '89 Fleer and Donruss Ken Griffey, Jr., cards — currently retail in the $10-12 range.

Perhaps the widespread counterfeiting of recent $100+ cards has made dealers and collectors more wary in their purchases, making it difficult to sell phony cards. The counterfeiting of lower-value cards may be an attempt to steal money from people who assume nobody would go to the trouble and expense to fake a $10 card. This is an especially sleazy ploy because it is more likely to defraud young collectors whose card-buying budgets tend more toward $10 cards than $100 cards.

Because there does not appear to be an immediate end in sight to the problem of card counterfeiting, we urge all readers to take advantage of the counterfeit update service offered on Page 2.

To help expose counterfeit cards quickly and prevent hobbyists from being defrauded, persons who encounter fakes which are not listed in this book are urged to contact the editor, Bob Lemke, at 700 E. State St., Iola, WI 54990, or by phoning 1-715-445-2214 during business hours.

Only by showing counterfeiters that the hobby is willing to work together to kill the market for their fakes will it be possible to eradicate this threat.

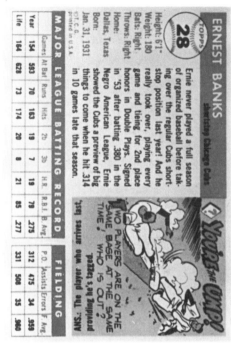

Because it is printed on thinner, whiter cardboard than the genuine 1955 Topps cards, an experienced dealer or collector should be able to spot this counterfeit with relative ease, especially when viewed outside of a plastic holder.

The presence of dot structures where they should not be provides conclusive evidence against the counterfeit, but does require a magnifying glass to verify.

The player's name, position and team at the bottom of the card and the facsimile autograph are the best places to examine a suspect card. On a genuine card, these elements will appear as clean, solid red or black lines. The counterfeit shows these elements as being made up of many tiny dots.

Likewise, the Cubs logo on the counterfeit shows dark dot patterns in the

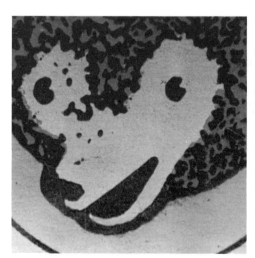

Genuine

Counterfeit

Counterfeit

white part of the bear's face and in the
surrounding yellow shield. On a genuine
card, these areas are free of dots.

The back of the counterfeit card is a

fairly good representation of the original,
except the black stats are much heavier
than on a genuine card.

Counterfeit

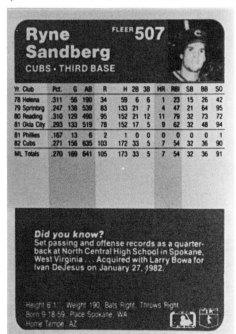

Yr. Club	Pct.	G	AB	R	H	2B	3B	HR	RBI	SB	BB	SO
78 Helena	.311	56	190	34	59	6	6	1	23	15	26	42
79 Sprtnbrg	.247	138	538	83	133	21	7	4	47	21	64	95
80 Reading	.310	129	490	95	152	21	12	11	79	32	73	72
81 Okla City	.293	133	519	78	152	17	5	9	62	32	48	94
81 Phillies	.167	13	6	2	1	0	0	0	0	0	0	1
82 Cubs	.271	156	635	103	172	33	5	7	54	32	36	90
ML Totals	.270	169	641	105	173	33	5	7	54	32	36	91

This is one of the few counterfeits which can be definitively detected with the naked eye. Unfortunately, the characteristic which allows this diagnosis cannot be differentiated in black-and-white photos. In fact, that characteristic *is* a black-and-white photo. On this counterfeit, the small portrait of Sandberg at the upper-right on the back is printed in black-and-white, instead of the sepia-and-white with which genuine 1983 Fleer cards present the back photo.

The typography on the front will provide additional evidence of counterfeit status. Genuine cards will show the red ''FLEER'' and the black player's name and position as solid letters. On the counterfeit, these letters are made up of many tiny dots, rendering a fuzzy appearance.

Similarly, the black and white lines which frame the photo on a genuine card are clean and crisp. On the counterfeit,

Genuine

Counterfeit

the black line shows fuzzy edges, while the white line has tiny dark dots invading it.

Likewise, the red "Cubs" in the logo is solid on a genuine, but comprised of red dots on the counterfeit. The registration mark (®) under the "s" of "Cubs" is clear and readable on a genuine card, but inde-cipherable on the counterfeit.

Returning to the back of card, the observer will note that the Major League and Players' Association logos at bottom-right have wording that is illegible on the counterfeit, even when viewed under magnification.

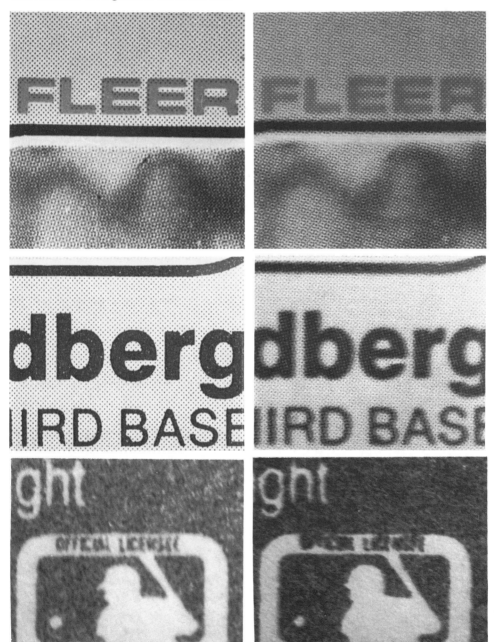

Genuine   **Counterfeit**

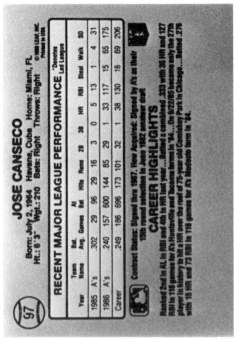

With any genuine 1987 Donruss card available for comparison, this counterfeit would fool no one. The top and bottom jet black borders of an original card appear on this counterfeit in a charcoal gray tone. Similarly, the colors of the player photo have a washed-out appearance.

Examination with a magnifying glass reveals that many of the design details which are present on a genuine card as clear, solid elements are represented on the counterfeit as fuzzy creations comprised of many tiny dots.

On a genuine card the Donruss logo will be made up of solid black letters and red numerals and the white area around the logo will be free from dots. The counterfeit shows the letters and the baseball to be made up of many tiny black dots which create a fuzzy appearance and spill over into the white outline. Similarly, the red "87" on a good card is clean and sharp, while the counterfeit displays the number as a pattern of tiny dots.

Like the baseball in the Donruss logo, the balls in the left and right borders on a

Genuine

Counterfeit

genuine card will be shown as clean black lines. On the counterfeit, these balls are made up of small dots, giving them a fuzzy look.

The green stripe near the bottom of a genuine 1987 Donruss Canseco rookie card ends cleanly at the edges of each letter of the player's name and position. On the counterfeit, green dots intrude into the edges of each of these letters.

Because the A's logo on a genuine card is comprised of a dot structure to give it color, it cannot be easily used as a counterfeit detector.

The back of the counterfeit card dis-

plays black type that is heavier than on a genuine card, causing some of the letters and numerals to run together in the area of the biographical data and "Career Highlights".

It can be noted, though not used as a counterfeit detector, that this fake has the back printing in factory-set orientation. That is, when the card is flipped over, the number appears in the lower-left corner. This is also true of genuine factory-set Canseco rookies. The wax pack version shows the card number on back in the upper-right corner when the card is flipped.

Genuine

Counterfeit

Unfortunately, the easiest way to spot this counterfeit doesn't show up well in a photograph, but we'll describe it anyway. Genuine 1989 Donruss cards have a "fifth color" ink — a flat black — that appears as a series of eight short horizontal bars in the black side borders to the left and right of the player photo. On this counterfeit, there are no bars visible.

When examined with a magnifying glass, the typographical elements on the front will provide additional evidence. Genuine cards will show the white letters of the player's name and position as having crisp edges which end cleanly at the purple background. On the counterfeit, there are many purple dots muddying up the edges of the letters.

On a real card, the blue "Rated Rookie", the red "Donruss" and the black "'89" are made up of solid colors. On the counterfeit, these elements are seen to

Genuine

Counterfeit

be composed of tiny dots. Many stray dots also appear in the white vertical pinstripes on the counterfeit's border.

The counterfeit also displays a very weak trademark ("TM") symbol to the right of the Rated Rookie logo. On a genuine card these letters are clean black lines.

The back of the counterfeit has Major League Baseball and MLB Players' Association logos that are considerably darker and less distinct than on a genuine card. The wording on the MLB logo at left is indecipherable on the counterfeit.

While such a judgement is subjective, it can be noted that the orange printing on the back of the counterfeit is more yellow than on a genuine card. It is also worth noting that the counterfeit features factory-set orientation of front and back. That is, when flipped over, the counterfeit will display the card number in the lower-left corner. Since a genuine factory-set Griffey card will display this same orientation, that trait cannot be considered a definitive indicator of a forgery. A wax-pack Griffey, when flipped from front to back, will show the card number at the upper-right.

Genuine   **Counterfeit**

At press time, Fleer had rendered an opinion that a 1989 Ken Griffey, Jr., card has been determined to be counterfeit.

Further details and photos were unavailable in time to include in this edition.

Since this counterfeit is believed to be the work of the same person who counterfeited the '89 Donruss Griffey card, reference to that listing should provide some useful information for persons confronted with a suspicious '89 Fleer Griffey card.

Particularly expect to see, under mag-

nification, dot structures on the counterfeit that do not appear on the original card. Good places to check would include the Mariners logo and "TM" trademark symbol at upper-right and the "FLEER" logo at lower-right on the front.

On the back, check the Major League Baseball and Players' Associations logos for legibility.

Detail photos of a genuine card are presented here for comparison to suspected counterfeits.

Genuine

Genuine

Genuine

If you buy a counterfeit

What do you do if you discover that you have a counterfeit card in your collection, portfolio or inventory?

Realistically, you are probably not going to be able to recoup your purchase price, much less the current value of the card. This is especially true if your card was bought at a card show or flea market, where counterfeits flourish and sellers tend to be itinerants or part-timers. Even if you know from whom you bought the card, it is unlikely they will accept your word that your counterfeit is the same card they sold you.

If you bought a counterfeit from a local shop owner, or a reputable dealer in one of the card publications, you may have better luck in getting reimbursed. The seller's willingness to make good will likely be in direct proportion to how valuable of a customer you have been in the past, and the esteem in which he holds his reputation. Again, there may be problems convincing even the most reputable dealer that a card you bought months or years ago is his responsibility.

Please resist the urge, if you can't get your money back from the seller, to pass the fake on to another unsuspecting victim. Doing so makes you as unscrupulous as the original counterfeiter and if you get caught, your own reputation will be shattered — along with your nose, possibly.

Since you can't recoup your fiscal losses, you might be tempted to seek justice in the criminal system, but the cold facts are that it is unlikely you will have any success in putting the counterfeiter or seller behind bars. Persons who make or sell phony bubblegum cards are not in the same league with those who deal crack in schoolyards. In most jurisdictions neither the police nor the prosecutor's office will give much priority to what really amounts in most cases to petit larceny.

As mentioned in an earlier chapter, a few of the card companies are starting to pursue counterfeiters, but their interest seems to be limited to finding the original source of the counterfeits. They are unlikely to assist the individual who has been stuck with a fake card or two.

If you find you've been stuck with one of the counterfeits detailed in this book, the best thing you can do is permanently mark it as such by writing on the back and giving it a place of ''honor'' in your collection as a conversation piece.

To help expose counterfeit cards quickly and prevent hobbyists from being defrauded, persons who encounter fakes which are not listed in this book are urged to contact the editor, Bob Lemke, at 700 E. State St., Iola, WI 54990, or by phoning 1-715-445-2214 during business hours.